教育的跨文化性

Fred Dervin 著　　袁梅　张莞 译

中央民族大学出版社
China Minzu University Press

图书在版编目（CIP）数据

教育的跨文化性 /（芬）弗雷德·德文（Fred Dervin）著；袁梅，张莞译．
—北京：中央民族大学出版社，2020.12（2021.5 重印）
（民族教育与全球化丛书）
ISBN 978-7-5660-1823-6

Ⅰ．①教… Ⅱ．①弗… ②袁… ③张… Ⅲ．①教育学—研究 Ⅳ．① G40
中国版本图书馆 CIP 数据核字（2020）第 179479 号

First published in English under the title
Interculturality in Education: A Theoretical and Methodological Toolbox
by Fred Dervin

教育的跨文化性

著　　者　Fred Dervin
译　　者　袁　梅　张　莞
责任编辑　赵　鹏
封面设计　舒刚卫
出版发行　中央民族大学出版社
　　　　　北京市海淀区中关村南大街 27 号　　邮编：100081
　　　　　电话：（010）68472815（发行部）　传真：（010）68933757（发行部）
　　　　　　　　（010）68932218（总编室）　　　　（010）68932447（办公室）
经 销 者　全国各地新华书店
印 刷 厂　北京鑫宇图源印刷科技有限公司
开　　本　787×1092　1/16　　印张：10.75
字　　数　132 千字
版　　次　2020 年 12 月第 1 版　2021 年 5 月第 2 次印刷
书　　号　ISBN 978-7-5660-1823-6
定　　价　58.00 元

序 言

声不过五，五声之变，不可胜听也；

色不过五，五色之变，不可胜观也；

味不过五，五味之变，不可胜尝也。

——孙武《孙子兵法》

我们身边的多样性无处不在，世界各国各地皆是如此，并无例外。开篇引用《孙子兵法》的优雅辞句恰好表达了这种复杂而又统一的多样性：我们的所听所见所闻常常只是世界多样性的缩影。对社会人而言，多样性不仅包括孙武提到的声色味（对于声音、颜色和味道的不同感受），还包括但不限于性别、年龄、民族和语言等。在中国，我们的多样性形成了统一性的基础。

目前，教育中的多样性已经成为所有教育者、学者和政策制定者最关注的问题，教育研究和实践领域的大多数超国家组织，从经济合作与发展组织（OECD）到联合国教科文组织（UNESCO），都一直提醒着我们关注教育中的多样性。但这从来不是轻而易举之事，即便大多数国家可能都已采用了不同视角和途径来面对教育中的多样性问题。

尽管从事民族教育研究多年，我总会自问该如何进一步推动中国的教育多样性和公平性。通过多年来的教学、研究工作，我发现在教育多样性和公平性领域我们仍面临许多难题，但也不乏成功的案例和值得引以为鉴的好做法。

每当参加国际会议或出国进行学术访问时，我也会与外国学者讨论这些问题，并向他们介绍中国民族教育研究领域已取得的进展。通过与他们的交谈，我意识到某些西方盛行的观点并不总适用于中国，甚至也不适用于世界其他国家或地区。尽管有些观点发人深省，但它们却源于不同的意识形态和社会背景。

在与外国学者的接触中让我明白，他们中的许多人实际上对中国的现实知之甚少，特别是民族教育方面。

本书的作者是我及我在中央民族大学团队的亲密合作伙伴。自三年前相识以后，我们便一起开展合作研究，发表论文，共同组织国内外的学术活动，并就Fred称之为多元教育的目标、优势和方法不断进行讨论。多元教育其实是一个概括性术语，描述的是如何在教育机构中实现多元个体的存在和互动，也被称之为文化间性的、多文化的、跨文化的或全球的教育。相处之中，Fred惊讶于我们在民族教育方面做的工作。他说自己确实没有了解过这样的多元教育方式，并对我们的研究和想法给予高度肯定。他自称，在跨文化领域寻觅多年后，终于遇到了民族教育——一种不同以往的、针对教育多样性的别样思考方式，是对以往权威（西方主流思想）的挑战，令人为之一振。

Fred知识渊博，求知欲强，对多元教育相关问题充满了真挚的研究之心。他充分认识到中国民族教育和芬兰移民的跨文化教育在社会背景上的不同，当然，通过我们的合作，他还是发现了二者的许多相似之处，比如两国学校中都有一些良好做法，丰富了教育多样性的视角。对于如何使用和翻译多元教育中的某些概念和定义，我们也反复讨论了很多次。正如Fred所指出的，许多术语无法被译入另一种语言，原因在于，某一术语在不同语境中有不同的含义。因此，在合作过程中，我们重新商定了跨文化教育领域的一些关键概念。Fred是位谨慎而谦逊的学者，他希望通过彼此的合作，双方能够真正受益，增进知识，促进交流，改进方法。

我们推介的这本书具有重要意义。此书在西方的出版发行，标志着跨文化教育在讨论方式、问题化研究和教学手段等方面都发生了改变。全书呈现了Fred对教育多样性是什么的思考，条分缕析，发人深省。他在书中提出了许多问题同时也给出了令人信服的答案。他犀利的观点可以帮助我们反思自己对跨文化性的已有认知，反思目前我们在跨文化研究和教学中使用的相关概念和方法。Fred建议读者跳脱藩篱，不要将目光只局限于他提出的“西方”学界如何研究跨文化性的问题，非常具有魄力，相信会给读者带来启发。

目前中国许多学者使用的概念、定义和方法，基本都来自西方语境。尽管在中国语境尝试使用无可厚非，Fred却鼓励我们审慎观察、大胆质疑，必要时对这些概念、定义和方法进行修正，以便更好地为我所用。Fred同时也建议，如有必要，读者大可考虑摒弃其中的某些因素。

在过去几年的时光里，Fred与我及民大团队成员合作的过程中，他曾一次又一次告诉我们，他正在经历的是跨文化思考的新革命。对我们而言，过去几年的合作也具有重要意义，我很高兴双方能够互相理解与支持。更令人欣慰的是，我们得以将同事和朋友们完成的重要研究成果向更多的中国读者推广。Fred一直是一位非常真诚的学者，与他的合作也十分愉快。在此，我谨借用文学家Philip Dormer Stanhope（1694—1773）歌颂友谊的话语作结:“真正的友谊是慢慢增长起来的，决不会突如其来，除非已有深入了解，相互看重。”相互看重是跨文化交际的关键词，国际学术圈比以往任何时候都更需要相互看重。这本书是Fred和我及我的团队多年合作的成果。希望读者阅读此书时亦能从我们的成果中受益！

苏德

2020年7月9日

Bibliography

STANHOPE P. D. Letters Written by the Late Right Honourable Philip Dormer Stanhope, Earl of Chesterfield, to His Son Philip Stanhope, Esq. Volume 1[M]. London: J. Dodsley, 1775.

SUN TZU. The Art of War[M]. Minneapolis: Filiquarian Publishing, LLC, 2007.

Foreword

Sude

> There are not more than five musical notes, yet the combinations of these five give rise to more melodies than can ever be heard.
>
> There are not more than five primary colours, yet in combination they produce more hues than can ever been seen.
>
> There are not more than five cardinal tastes, yet combinations of them yield more flavours than can ever be tasted.
>
> Sun Tzu (*The Art of War*)

Diversity is all around us, in every country around the world, there are simply no exceptions. Sun Tzu's beautiful opening words translate well this complexity: what we hear, what we see, what we smell is always just a limited version of the diversity of our world. For us social beings, our diversity includes all the elements mentioned by Sun Tzu (the way we sound, our colours, our special brands of human smell) but also (amongst others) gender, age, ethnicity and language. In China, our diversity forms the basis of our unity.

Dealing with diversity in education is an issue that all educators, scholars and decision-makers have to prioritize today and most supranational institutions that deal with education research and practice remind us to do so, from the OECD to the UNESCO. However, it is not an easy task and different countries might adopt specific approaches and perspectives to do so.

As one of the top specialists in Minzu education, I often ask myself the question of how to promote further inclusion of diversity and education justice in China. Through my writings, research and involvement with training educators, I have identified some of the challenges that we face here, but also some successes, and some 'good' practices that we can learn from.

At international conferences and during my research stays abroad (e.g. US, UK, Finland) I have also dialogued with foreign scholars about these issues and tried to promote the work that we have been doing in diversity education in China to them. Through the dialogues I have had with them, I realized that some of the ideas that are prevalent for e.g. in the West are not always adapted to our Chinese context – or even to other parts of the world. These ideas are often fascinating but they derive from different ideologies and societal contexts.

During my encounters with foreign scholars I have also realized that knowledge about the Chinese context is limited, especially in relation to Minzu education.

The author of this book is a close cooperator with my team at Minzu University of China. We met three years ago and have had the opportunity to cooperate on research and publications, organize joint events abroad and in China and dialoguing around the goals, benefits and approaches to what Dervin calls

Diversity Education — an umbrella term that refers to different approaches to the presence of and interaction of diverse individuals in institutions of education, which might be labelled as intercultural, multicultural, transcultural, global education. When we met, Fred was impressed by the work that we do in Minzu education. He admitted that he was not aware of this kind of approach to diversity and praised our research and ideas. For Fred, Minzu education was what he had been looking for for years: an alternative, stimulating and challenging, different way of thinking about diversity in education.

Fred is a very curious and knowledgeable scholar, and a scholar who is genuinely interested in dialogue and exchange about these issues. Of course, he is well aware of the differences in contexts (Minzu education in China versus migrant-intercultural education in Finland), however through our collaboration we have been able to identify similarities for instance in terms of practices in schools that have enriched both of our perspectives on diversity in education. We have also had many discussions on how to use and translate concepts and notions to discuss this kind of education. As he notes rightly, many of these terms are untranslatable in different languages since they don't have the same connotations. Thus, through our cooperation we have renegotiated some of the key concepts of the field of intercultural education. Fred is a very careful scholar who has humility and he wants to make sure that through our cooperation we all benefit genuinely in terms of knowledge, scientific interactions and methodologies.

The book that we introduce here is a very important one. When the book was published in the West, it marked a turning point in the way intercultural education was discussed, problematized and taught. The book presents in a very clear and stimulating way Dervin's ideas about what diversity in education could be. He does ask a lot of questions but also presents convincing answers. His arguments are sharp and he helps us to revise some of our assumptions about interculturality, the concepts that go with it as well as methods that have been used to research and teach about it. Dervin's proposals to go beyond the problems that he has identified with how interculturality is 'done' in the West are groundbreaking and will inspire the reader.

Many of us in China use concepts and notions but also methods that come from Western contexts. Although there is no problem in testing them out in the Chinese context, what Fred empowers us to do is to examine these elements carefully, to question them and — at times — to modify them so we can make use of them in better ways. Fred also suggests doing away with some of these elements, which the reader is free to consider too.

Fred has said repeatedly that over the last years of cooperation with my team and I, he has experienced a new revolution of intercultural thinking. These years have also been important to us and I am delighted that we can both support each other. I am even more delighted that we can promote our colleague and friend's important work to Chinese audiences. Fred has been a very generous scholar to work with, and I would like to finish with a quote from the man of letters Philip Dormer Stanhope (1694-1773) who said about friendship: "Real friendship is a flow grower; and never thrives, unless ingrafted upon a stock of known and reciprocal merit". Reciprocity is a keyword in intercultural encounters and it is needed more than ever in international academia. This book bears the fruits of "reciprocal merit" between Fred, my team and I. May the reader also reap these fruits while reading the book!

Bibliography

STANHOPE P. D. Letters Written by the Late Right Honourable Philip Dormer Stanhope, Earl of Chesterfield, to His Son Philip Stanhope, Esq. Volume 1[M]. London: J. Dodsley, 1775.

SUN TZU. The Art of War[M]. Minneapolis: Filiquarian Publishing, LLC, 2007.

中文版序言

我不懂人们为什么惧怕新想法。（而）我恐惧的是旧观点。

——Jonh Cage（2003：21）。

这本书的中文版本能与大家见面，我感到十分高兴。首先，我想借此机会感谢中央民族大学教育学院袁梅副教授及其同事们为此做出的努力，他们的工作非常出色。在此，真心希望此书能够促使读者以一种全新的方式，去反思和讨论跨文化性到底是什么、跨文化性又会带来什么。

这本书是我作为跨文化交际教育学者生涯中的一个重要节点，因为书中提出的颇具争议性的跨文化性概念，是我与其斗争、纠结多年后得出的最新观点。

在此篇中文版的序言中，我想说明为什么我的中国读者需要阅读这本书，并建议读者如何将此书当作一本工具书，将跨文化性概念付诸实践。我建议读者们读两次序言，一次在阅读全书内容之前，一次在阅读全书内容之后，因为这篇序言不仅是对全书的介绍，也算是总结。同时，它也会让读者仔细思考接下来要读的内容，思考阅读此书将给您带来的收获。

事实上，跨文化性（interculturality）这个词是近期才在英语语言中使用的。15年前，受到法国学术圈的影响，我将这个词引介到了全球跨文化交际教育的圈子。这个词由两部分组成：inter-表示相互关系、中间性和相互作用，通俗说就是两人或两人以上之间发生的事；-culturality的本质是文化概念，但-ality的后缀表明了一种过程，一种反复不断讨论协商的过程。所以首要的也是最重要的，跨文化性是在人与人之间发生的、永无止境的过程，所以我们在分析跨文化性时需要把所有的对话者都考虑在内。文化在这里指的并不是通常使用的概念，而是本书中所解释的超越了“国家”的概念。简而言之，可用Deleuze（2011：n.p.）的话来概括：“从某种程度上说我并不相信文化，但我相信接触。”人与人之间的接触总是第一位的，而非文化。

最近，我也遭遇了生命中最震撼的一次接触。那时我身处芬兰的一片森林里，坚持着新冠疫情期间的每日散步。森林很空旷，周围连人影也没有。突然，我遇到了一只非常大的麋鹿，它站在离我也就四五米的地方，目测有600公斤重。芬兰全境大概有10万只麋鹿。这只麋鹿看到我后愣住了。那一刻，我也僵住了。我们一动不动，互相对视。这种局面持续了将近10分钟。我惊讶于这只动物如此耐心，思考着它盯着我却不与我交流时到底在想些什么。森林的寂静和偶尔的几声鸟鸣，也增加了几丝趣味。我就站在那里，面对如此的庞然大物，我们就这样对视，其他什么也不做。麋鹿似乎在上上下下打量着我。我也一样打量着它。几分钟后我突然想到：这是不是就有点像跨文化性？每当我们与其他国家的人“闲聊”时，我们其实只是在打量彼此，并没有真正在交流什么。我经常发现自己身处这样的情景：有人在问完我“你来自哪里”后，我的对话者常会抛给我关于“我的”国家的最差的陈词滥调和固化印象，比如他们认为我是“芬兰”人，但其实芬兰人只是一部分的我，以及关于芬兰是个快乐的国家这样与现实不符的固化印象。我就静静听着，不愿打断或回应他们。我敢肯定，在以往的人生经历中，我对很多遇到的人都是这么做的。我觉得这次与麋鹿的接触与那些“跨文化”接触非常类似，都是对视片刻，然后分道扬镳。

Jules Verne 1870年出版的小说《环游月球》（*Around the moon*）中的人物亚尔当（Arden）曾感叹道：“有多少事物是从未知世界而来的啊!”这也是我想借此书传达给中国读者的第一个信息：我们确实对跨文化交际教育领域正在发生的一切知之甚少。尽管自20世纪70年代以来，全世界都在进行跨文化交际教育研究和实践，可我们不是被某些曾指导了研究工作的意识形态所误导（比如新自由主义、文化主义），就是对发生在来自不同国家或不同“文化”的两个人之间的一切了解得并不透彻。跨文化首要和最重要的是人与人的接触，而这还有待我们继续探索和深究。

无知不尽然是件坏事。首先这意味着我们还有很多重要的工作要做，因此无知成为了一个良好的起点和机遇。其次，如Corbin（2020）坚信的那样，因为无知我们才有梦可做，去梦想更美好的世界、更有效的交流和更完善的教育。但正如此书中提出的，只有当我们开始对跨文化性的方方面面进行系统的批判性思考时，无知才会变成好事。Camus（1962：41）说过，我们的大脑必须“监督自己”。最近几年已有很多关于批判性思维的论述，讨论其在教育和研究中的重要作用。令人遗憾的是，批判性思维观点的使用效果却并不尽如人意。每个人似乎都想要变得批判，或声称自己是批判的，但其实对批判性的含义并不确定。当您阅读这本书时，我向您保证，您将会感受到批判性是如何系统而连贯地发挥作用的。我理解的批判性与Paul（2008：n.p.）的部分观点不谋而合：“批判性思维是你在思考的同时思考你的思维方式，为了进行更好的思考。”我不同意这句话的后半句，因为我不相信思考能变得“更好”。思考会改变和进化，但“变得更好”却让我觉得是非常模糊的说法（为谁变得更好？谁来决定什么叫更好?）。而且“变得更好”会让我们太容易产生满足感而掉以轻心。我的原则是从来不完全满足于自己的思考。这个世界有时太复杂，有时又太简单。对我们这些教育者和学者来说，这个世界有太多太多的问题需要我们放手。还是如Camus所说，我们必须迫使我们的大脑监督自己，就算所有专家都认可你的观点！

这本书本来是受我在“西方”不同国家和马来西亚的过往经历的启发而作。写书的时候，我对中国的认识还仅限于中国南方以及北京的几次旅行。后来有机会在中国大陆生活了更长的时间后，我又发现了更多跨文化性的新内容，我的大脑又得以一遍又一遍地“监督自己”。通过与苏德教授、袁梅副教授及其团队成员在民族教育方面的共同研究，我发现跨文化性如同一只变色龙，会不断变换颜色。我认为中国的教育者和学者应该将目光投向中国古已有之并贯穿至今的多样性和跨文化交流，以此来启发他们对于跨文化交际教育的研究（见袁等，2020）。

下面这个譬喻可以用来理解跨文化性。就像折纸这门发源于中国的艺术，将一张平整的正方形纸张改造成复杂精细的设计作品，跨文化性也是对聚在一起工作学习、吃玩、相恋的人们的复杂解读。当我们一起做这些事时，人类交流互动的起伏变化也被重新塑造。就像折纸用的是一张薄薄的纸片，跨文化性也不是永恒不变的，而是随着人们的交流而不断变化。其实正如我在书中所述，跨文化性最重要的概念大概是身份。就像折纸时纸片被人从一张纸创造成不同样子，人们相见时在对方面前表现的自己，是在交流中形成的新样子，是不稳定的、非永久性的脆弱的身份。在跨文化交际领域运用多年的文化概念不足以描述复杂的身份，因为它偏向于用在更加简单化和静态化的情境中。况且也不是所有因素都与文化相关。跨文化性还包括诸如性别、社会地位、肤色等表征。

接下来我想要对如何实践跨文化性提一些建议。这些建议写于原书出版四年后，因此其中包含了一些可能有别于书中的新内容。当然，我希望当您下次阅读我的作品或在会议上听我发言时，又能再听到更新颖更不同的内容，这就说明我一直在身体力行地尝试着不断改变我们“干”跨文化的方式。如果一个人对跨文化性的思考方式不随时间而变化，这其实是思维上的懒惰和不诚实。作为教育者和学者，我们的目标是不断提供新工具，去思考和理解跨文化性，去实践跨文化性的新观点。

1. 跨文化性是一个意识形态上的概念，从不同社会、经济和政治视角反映出我们是谁和他们是谁。因此，我们必须时刻注意每一种研究和实践跨文化性的方法所产生的背景：这是谁的观点？他们用了什么概念？产生于世界何处？我能在观点之后发现作者和/或机构的什么？这些观点是否与我自己的信仰或我应该在教育中传播的观点一致？我们如何改造它们以更好地适用于我们自身？或是其中哪些内容应该被替代？比如在中国流传甚广的Michael Byram的思想其实是非常有问题的，因为他对跨文化性的思考方式是以欧洲为中心的（例如“跨文化公民身份”观点）。Michael Byram的研究是为欧洲理事会做的，而欧洲理事会带有明显政治色彩，因此很可能与中国教师思索中国跨文化交际的现实相冲突。同样有问题的还有所谓的跨文化能力模型。这些模型是在特定背景下以特定意识形态为指导而设计的，我们务必要时刻注意和警惕这一点。比如这些模型中包含了中国背景下不曾使用的概念（如种族），因此并不适用于中国。所以在盲目使用这些思想之前，我们必须慎之又慎，擦亮自己的双眼，重新看待跨文化性的复杂现实情况。我们最好把这个偏见也忘了：外国的月亮比中国的圆。

2. 鉴于研究和教育中的许多跨文化观点反映的都是所谓的西方意识形态，所以我们有必要搞清楚在中国背景下关于跨文化交际的研究有哪些进展。与中国同事的共同研究让我发现了民族教育，但我却好奇为什么研究跨文化性的中国学者不使用民族教育的观点。后来我意识到对于有些学者来说，跨文化只意味着跨国界。但对我而言跨文化并不仅限于此。跨文化也会在国内发生，发生在我们遇见的来自不同地区、不同文化背景的人之间。在中国，所有人的核心是相同的：国籍、历史、对中国人的身份认同和共同的语言等等。他们都是中国人。但在相同的中国人身份之外，有些人可能说不同的方言或语言，吃不同的食物，或来自大城市或来自小乡镇等。这些也让中国具有了多样性和跨文化性，因为当这些人见面时他们需要去交流并展示自己身份的某些方面。但这只是一方面。在我看来，古老的中国哲学对于我们反思跨文化性非常重要。想想儒家思想吧！过去几年我重新阅读《论语》后，才明白自己被西方思想"洗脑"，误解了孔子思想，对其中许多道理的认知是完全错误的。比如孔子强调的不断的自我完善和持续的社会交流，对跨文化而言就至关重要。1972年Fingarette写道："我越来越确定地相信，时至今日，孔子依然可以成为我们的老师，而且是一位主流老师，不只是在主流观点之外为我们带来一些异域视角的老师。他所传授的知识独一无二，不可或缺。他带来了新思想。"在我最近发表的文章中，我解释了被西方思想误读了的儒家学说，如何成为改变我们对跨文化性理解方式的主要推手（Dervin，2020）。虽然您即将阅读或已经读完的书，主要是基于"西方的"观点，但请记住，此刻我们必须超越这些观点。中国本土的思想家和教育者，无论古今，已经形成了对重新思考跨文化性至关重要的思想。请心存好奇！请阅读它们！请试试他们的想法！看看他们的观点是否能与现行的跨文化观点相结合，亦或是能够丰富关于跨文化的讨论。我们能从彼此（“东方”和“西方”）之间学到什么，以此来重新探讨该如何理解我们的关系？“东方”世界尝试着了解自己，却被要求使用“西方”的观点和方法才能与其沟通交流，这似乎愈加显出了不公。我一直很欣赏Joseph Needham对中国的热爱，当然我本人也很爱中国。他的话也对研究跨文化有一定启示：“中华文明拥有如全然的他者般令人无法抗拒的魅力，而只有全然的他者才会激发起最深沉的爱意和最强大的动力，去学习。”（Needham，1969：176）

3.我的最后一点建议是，当我们尝试着理解跨文化性而将目光投向别人时，我们不妨先回望一下自己。Roland Barthes（2012）在其关于中国的书中，一直将他在中国看到的一切与法国做对比，最后发现了中法之间许多相同之处。书中他在观察中国人时提出了一个重要观点：“我觉得我一点也弄不懂他们，我只是在通过他们弄懂我们自己。所以我要写的并不是‘所以中国是什么’，而是‘所以法国是什么’。”（2012：57）向内看与向外看同样重要。在上文提到的我与麋鹿相遇的10分钟里，我的内心上演了无数关于自己的心理活动（以人为中心）：这只麋鹿觉得我好看不好看？他/她觉得我聪明还是愚蠢？他/她会好奇我的习惯和行为吗？他/她会因为我是人类而可怜我吗？我每天的交际与这次交际有什么相似之处吗？向内看可以让我们更好地了解自身的复杂性和矛盾性，同时也认识到我们遇到的每一个个体都如我们自身一样复杂，他们有着自己的矛盾，表现出不同的身份，有缺点也有优点。只有这样做，我们才算真正开始认识他人，不再以过于简化的视角评价他们。因为通过简化视角看到的未必真实（就像我们自己在表现角色和行为，他们也是）。向内看还包括带着批判性思维去反思翻译的运用。我们在写作或讨论跨文化性时所使用的大多数术语，特别是外文术语，基本上都来自另一个语境。这些词有不同的内涵和外延，因此对我们自身的现实而言是“无法译入的”。在中国的几年我发现了很多这样的词，比如宽容（tolerance）、异域（exotic）、文明（civilization）、天赋（talent）等，在我看来语意很“明确”，但这些词在中文中经常是一词多义的，其所指含义与我所知道的其他（欧洲）语言并不相同。因此翻译时我们必须十分谨慎，思考这些词语运用在另一种语言的教育和研究背景中时有没有多种（隐藏的）含义。帮助学生首先明白这一点也是很重要的。

中国发明了被称为“魔镜”的铜镜。最后，我想以魔镜作比，说明跨文化作为教育目标到底意味着什么。镜子的背面是浮雕设计（比如中国的十二生肖）。镜子的正面平滑光洁，起到镜子的功能。如果让光线照射在镜面上，光线会反射在一片空白墙面上，那么你会发现镜背的花纹会映现在空白墙面上。跨文化就是用这样一面镜子，让光照射在镜面上，这样我们既能看到镜面里的自己和镜背后的一面（比如来自别国的人），带着批判性和反思性去同时看待自己和他人。这是在2020年的开端提出的一个有趣建议，而全世界范围内的新冠疫情危机证明，这也许是终结民族中心主义（相信自己才是最好的、过度自信）、种族歧视（结构性种族歧视或隐藏在文化评价之后的歧视）以及差别待遇的重要手段。前路漫漫，荆棘丛生，但我们仍应心存感激，感恩还有机会去探索跨文化性的新的思考方式。希望此书能为此做出些许贡献。

参考文献

BARTHES R. Travels in China [M]. Cambridge：Polity Press, 2012.

CAGE J. Conversing with Cage [M]. London：Routledge, 2003.

CAMUS A. Notebooks 1935 — 1942 [M]. New York：Knopf, 1962.

CORBIN A. Terra Incognita：Une Histoire de l' Ignorance [M]. [Terra Incognita：A History of Ignorance]. Paris：Albin Michel, 2020.

DELEUZE G. Gilles Deleuze from A to Z. DVD [M]. Cambridge: MA：MIT Press, 2011.

DERVIN F. Creating and combining models of Intercultural Competence for teacher education/training: On the need to rethink IC frequently [M]// DERVIN F.，MOLONEY R. & SIMPSON A.（Eds.）. Intercultural Competence in the Work of Teachers. London：Routledge, 2020: 57-71.

FINGARETTE H. Confucius：The Secular as Sacred [M]. New York：Harper, 1972.

NEEDHAM J. The Grand Titration：Science and Society in East and West [M]. London：Routledge, 1969.

PAUL R. Critical thinking：Basic questions and answers [EB/OL]. http：//www.criticalthinking.org.

VERNE J. All Around the Moon [M]. Loschberg：Jazzybee Verlag, 1870.

YUAN M.，SUDE，WANG T.，ZHANG W.，CHEN N.，SIMPSON A. & DERVIN F. Chinese minzu education in higher education：An inspiration for 'Western' diversity education [J]. British Journal of Educational Studies, 2020.

Foreword to the Chinese edition

> I can't understand why people are frightened of new ideas. I'm frightened of the old ones.
>
> John Cage (2003: 21)

I am delighted that this book now appears in Chinese and I would like to take this opportunity to thank Prof. Yuan Mei and her colleagues for making this happen. They have done an amazing job and I do hope that the book will start conversations about what interculturality is and what it could entail, maybe beyond the usual ways of thinking about it.

This book was an important point in my career as a scholar in intercultural communication education as it represented the most up-to-date publication that reflected my views on the thorny notion of interculturality, after years of struggle with it.

In this foreword to the Chinese edition, I would like to explain why reading this book is important for my Chinese readers and to give some suggestions as to how we can move forward with the notion, using the book as a toolbox for that purpose. I suggest the foreword is read first and, again, after reading the entire book, as it serves, in a sense, as both an updated introduction and conclusion to the book. At the same time, it allows you the reader to reflect on what you are about to read and what you will get from reading the book.

The notion of interculturality has been used only just recently in English. I introduced it to the global field of intercultural communication education 15 years ago, influenced by the way the word has been used in French academic circles. The word is composed of two terms: inter- which refers to relations, betweenness, interaction (something that is happening between two people or more) and -culturality has the concept of culture as its roots, but is complemented by -ality which suggests a process, something that is negotiated again and again. So interculturality is first and foremost something that takes place between people (which means that we need to consider ALL interlocutors when we analyse interculturality) and that is a never-ending process. The concept of culture here does not refer to the usual meaning of the concept, and moves beyond the 'national', as is explained in this book. To make it simple here, I could refer to Deleuze (2011: n.p.), who said: "I don't believe in culture, to some extent, but rather I believe in encounters." Encounters between people are always first, never culture.

Recently, I made one of the most striking encounters of my life. I was in a forest in Finland, taking my daily walk during the COVID-19 crisis. The forest was empty, not a single human soul around. Suddenly I came across a very big elk (moose), which stood probably 2 meters and was about 600kg. In Finland there are about 100,000 elks. The elk froze when it saw me, standing just 4-5 meters away from me. I also froze. We stared at each other without moving. This lasted about 10 minutes. I was so impressed by the patience of this animal and started wondering what it was thinking about, staring at me, without any means of communicating with me. The silence of the forest, with just a few birds tweeting, was also interesting. There I was, facing a huge animal, the two of us just staring at each other, nothing else was happening. The elk seemed to observe every inch of my face and body. I was doing the same. After a few minutes I started wondering: is this somewhat a bit like interculturality? Often, when we 'chitchat' with people from other countries, in fact, we just stare at each other without really communicating. I have often found myself in such situations where, after asking me 'where are you from', my interlocutor throws at me the worst clichés and stereotypes about 'my' country (usually they think 'Finland' but that's just one part of who I am, and the stereotypical ideas of what Finland is — e.g. a happy nation — do not correspond at all to the reality). I then just listen silently, not willing to disturb them or to respond. I am sure that many times in my life I have done the same thing to the people I have met. The encounter with the elk was very similar to such 'intercultural' encounters, I think. We stared at each other for a while and then went our own ways.

In his novel *Around the moon* Jules Verne (1870) makes one of his characters say: "Oh what a lot of volumes," cried Ardan, "could be made out of what we don't know." This is the first message of this book to my Chinese reader: we are in fact pretty ignorant of what is happening in intercultural communication education. Although practice and research on this kind of education has been taking place in different parts of the world since the 1970s, either we have been misled by certain ideologies that guide our work (e.g. neoliberalism, culturalism) or we don't know enough to fully understand what is occurring when two people from different countries or 'cultures' meet. Interculturality is first and foremost about human encounters. And we still have a lot to learn about them too.

Our ignorance is not a bad thing as such. It means first and foremost that we still have a lot of important work to do. So, our ignorance is a good starting point and an opportunity. Second, as Corbin (2020) maintains, ignorance can still allow us to dream of a better world, better interactions and better education. Yet, as is argued in this book, this can only happen when we start thinking critically and systematically about interculturality — every aspect of it. As Camus (1962: 41) said, our mind must "watch itself". A lot has been written about critical thinking in recent years, and of its importance in education and research. Unfortunately, it appears that the idea of critical thinking is not always working well. It appears that everybody wants to be or is urged to be critical, but we are not always sure what it means. While reading this book, I promise that you the reader will get to see how criticality can function systematically and coherently. The way I understand criticality here is summarized partly by Paul (2008: n.p.): "Critical thinking is thinking about your thinking while you're thinking in order to make your thinking better." I disagree with the second part of the quote since I don't believe that our thinking can get 'better'. It can change and evolve but 'get better', I think, is a very unstable construct (Better for whom? Who decides what is better?). Besides 'get better' can give a too easy sense of satisfaction that might make us putting our guards down. My rule is never to be fully satisfied with what I think. The world is too complex and too simple at the same time. The world faces too many issues for us as educators and scholars to let go. Going back to Camus, we must force our mind to watch itself — even when we feel that all the experts agree!

This book was inspired essentially from my experiences in different parts of the 'West' and Malaysia at the time. When I wrote the book, my experiences of China were limited to the south of the country and a few trips to Beijing and Shanghai. Since I have been able to spend more time in Mainland China, I have discovered many new aspects of interculturality and allowed my mind to 'watch itself' again and again. Through the work that Prof. Sude, Prof. Mei Yuan and our teams have done on Minzu education, I have discovered that interculturality is like a chameleon, this reptile that is able to change colors. China, of course, has a long history of interculturality with the outside world but also from within its own borders. And I believe that Chinese educators and scholars should look into this diversity and the interactions that have taken place in the past and today as an inspiration for their work on intercultural communication education (see Yuan et al., 2020).

I propose that the following metaphor be used to understand interculturality. Like Origami (折り紙), the art of paper folding which originated from China, which transforms a flat square sheet of paper into intricate design, interculturality represents complex interpretations of people coming together to work, study, love, eat, have fun, etc. This ebb and flow of human interactions is re-shaped as we do all these things together. Like Origami, which is done with a fragile piece of material, paper, interculturality is not permanent, it changes as people interact. Actually, as I argue in the book, the most important concept for interculturality is probably identity. People perform who they are with others when they meet, and thus like Origami and the folds that one creates from flat paper, they negotiate new shapes, unstable, non-permanent and fragile identities. The concept of culture that has been used for decades in the field of intercultural communication cannot describe complex identities, as it tends to be used in a simplistic, static way. And not everything is about culture… interculturality also involves representations of gender, social status, skin colour, etc.

In what follows I wish to give some advice about how to approach interculturality. This was written four years after the original book was published, therefore some of the following aspects might be new and different from what is contained in the book. And, hopefully, next time you read my work or listen to me at a conference, you might hear something different and complementary, which shows that I am trying again and again to propose change in the way we 'do' interculturality. Actually, thinking about interculturality without changing one's ideas overtime, is a sign of intellectual laziness and dishonesty. Our goal as educators and scholars is to offer again and again new tools to think about, understand and try out new ideas about interculturality.

1. Interculturality is an ideological concept, which reflects different socio-economic-politico perspectives on who we are and on who they are. It is thus important to be aware of the background of any approach to interculturality: whose ideas are there? What concepts do they use? From which part of the world? What can I find out about the author and/or institution behind this perspective? Are they compatible with my own beliefs or those that I am supposed

to transmit in education? How could we make them fit better our own context? Or what should they be substituted with? For example, Michael Byram's ideologies, who have been used extensively in China, can be problematic because they translate a very Eurocentric way of thinking about interculturality (for ex. his idea of 'intercultural citizenship'). The work was done for the Council of Europe, an institution which has a very clear political agenda, which, again, may clash with the way Chinese teachers think about their own realities. The same goes with any so-called model of intercultural competence. They were designed in specific contexts, with specific ideologies, of which we must be aware and sometimes careful. For instance, they might include concepts that are not in use in our context (e.g. race) and thus they cannot function. So, we must think carefully before blindly adopting such ideas, and wear new 'glasses' to read the complex realities of interculturality. We might also want to forget about this bias: 外国的月亮比中国的圆 ...

2. Since many ideas about interculturality in research and education reflect so-called Western ideologies, it is important to look into what has been done in our own context in relation to encounters. When I discovered Minzu education through my colleagues, I wondered why the Chinese scholars who work on interculturality did not use these ideas. I then realized that for these scholars, intercultural means international only. For me interculturality does not need to be about that. Interculturality also takes place locally, with the different kinds of people whom we meet (from different regions, social backgrounds, etc.). In China, all citizens share the same core: nationality, history, respect of the Chinese identity, a common language, etc. They are all Chinese. Further to this

identity, some people might speak a different dialect or language, eat different food, come from a big city or a village, etc. This makes China also diverse and intercultural, in the sense that when these people meet they need to negotiate certain parts of their identity. But there is more, Chinese philosophy is ancient and is, I believe, very important for reflecting on interculturality. Think about Confucian ethics. Rereading the Analects of Confucius over the past few years has allowed me to understand that I had misunderstood Confucianism since I had been 'brainwashed' by the West to think about it in completely wrong terms. I had missed for example the emphasis on constant self-improvement and continuous social interaction, which are central to interculturality. In 1972, Fingarette (ibid.: vii) wrote: "Increasingly I have become convinced that Confucius can be a teacher to us today – a major teacher, not one who merely gives us a slightly exotic perspective on the ideas already current. He tells us things not being said elsewhere; things needing to be said. He has a new lesson to teach". In a recent article, I explained how Confucianism, beyond the misunderstandings created in the West, can be a major 'reformer' of the way we understand interculturality (Dervin, 2020). Although the book you are about to read, or finished reading, mainly relies on 'Western' ideas, bear in mind that we must now look beyond these. Local Chinese thinkers and educators from today or the past, have developed ideas that can be vital in rethinking the way we 'do' interculturality. Be curious! Read them! Test their ideas! See if their ideas can be combined with current ideas about interculturality, or if, alone, they can enrich discussions around the notion. What is it that we can learn with each other (the 'East' with 'the West') so we can renegotiate how we understand our relations? It seems increasingly unfair that the 'East' tries to understand itself and how it interacts with the 'West' by asking the 'East' to use 'Western' ideas and methods. I have always admired Joseph Needham for his great love for China — a love I share — and what he says here, must inspire us for interculturality too: "Chinese civilization has the overpowering beauty of the wholly other, and only the wholly other can inspire the deepest love and the profoundest desire to learn." (Needham, 1969: 176)

3. My last point refers to questions of going back to oneself when we try to understand interculturality, before looking into other people. In his book about China, Roland Barthes (2012) keeps comparing what he sees in the Middle Kingdom to France — actually finding many similarities between China and France. At some point in the book, he makes an important point while observing Chinese people: "I feel I won't be able to shed light on them in the least – just shed light on us by means of them. So, what needs to be written isn't So, what about China? but So, what about France?"(2012: 57) Looking inwards is as important as observing the other. In the episode with the elk that I told earlier, a lot of internal (humancentric) thoughts about myself took place for the 10 minutes that we 'spent' together: does this elk find me ugly or attractive? Does she/he think I am clever, stupid or something else? Does she/he wonder about my habits and behaviours? Does she/he pity me for being a human? What in my daily encounters resemble this encounter? etc. Looking inwards is a way of becoming more aware of our own complexity and contradictions and, at the same time, to learn to accept that any human being we encounter is as complex as we are ourselves, with their own contradictions, performed identities, good sides,

bad sides, etc. It is only through this practice that we can start meeting others, and maybe stop judging them in simple terms. Because what we see in the other may not be a reality (as much as we perform roles and habits, they also do). Looking inwards also involves using translation critically and reflexively. As such most terms we use when we write or talk about interculturality, especially in foreign languages, come from a different context. These words might have different meanings and connotations and as such be 'untranslatable' in our own reality. Throughout my years in China I have come across many such words, which I thought were 'obvious': tolerance, exotic, civilization, talent, etc. Often, I discovered that these words were polysemic in Chinese and that they did not connote the same way as in the other (European) languages that I know. We must thus translate carefully, thinking about the multiple (hidden) meanings these words might have in the languages that we use in education and research. Helping students to prioritize this is also important.

China has invented the so-called Chinese Magic Mirrors which are made of bronze. To finish, I would suggest that these mirrors are a great metaphor to explain what interculturality, as an educational goal, could be about. On the back of the mirror there is a design in relief (e.g. Chinese Signs of the Zodiac). The front of the mirror is smooth and polished, and works as a mirror. And if you shine a light onto the front surface of the mirror, and project the reflected light onto a blank surface, you will see the image of the design on the back of the mirror. Interculturality is about using this mirror with the light onto the front surface so we can see ourselves and what lies behind (e.g. a person from another country) and critically and reflexively consider self and other simultaneously.

This is one interesting approach in the early 2020s and the COVID-19 crisis around the world has showed that it might be an important one to put an end to ethnocentrism (believing we are the best, over self-confidence), all forms of racism (structural racism, racism hidden behind comments about culture for instance), and discrimination. The way forward is long and paved with obstacles, but we should be grateful to be given the opportunity to find new ways to think about interculturality. I hope this book can make a little contribution to change.

Bibliography

BARTHES R. (2012). Travels in China [M]. Cambridge: Polity Press, 2012.

CAGE J. Conversing with Cage [M]. London: Routledge, 2003.

CAMUS A. Notebooks 1935-1942 [M]. New York: Knopf, 1962.

CORBIN A. Terra Incognita: Une Histoire de l'Ignorance [M]. [Terra Incognita: A History of Ignorance]. Paris: Albin Michel, 2020.

DELEUZE G. Gilles Deleuze from A to Z. DVD [M]. Cambridge: MA: MIT Press, 2011.

DERVIN F. Creating and combining models of Intercultural Competence for teacher education/training. On the need to rethink IC frequently [M]// DERVIN F., MOLONEY R. & SIMPSON A. (Eds.). Intercultural Competence in the Work of Teachers. London: Routledge, 2020: 57-71.

FINGARETTE H. Confucius: The Secular as Sacred. New York: Harper, 1972.

NEEDHAM J. The Grand Titration: Science and Society in East and West

[M]. London: Routledge, 1969.

PAUL R. Critical thinking: Basic questions and answers [EB/OL]. http://www.criticalthinking.org.

VERNE J. All Around the Moon [M]. Loschberg: Jazzybee Verlag, 1870.

YUAN M., SUDE, WANG T., ZHANG W., CHEN N., SIMPSON A. & DERVIN F. Chinese minzu education in higher education: An inspiration for 'Western' diversity education [J] British Journal of Educational Studies, 2020.

目　录

第一章　引言

——教育中的跨文化性：新起点？

摘　要：本章中，笔者阐述了为什么要重新思考跨文化性在当今教育中的作用。笔者认为，“跨文化性”这一概念的内涵有时过于丰富，有时却又过于贫乏，这说明其内涵具有多义性。因此迫切需要为“跨文化性”赋予新的含义，使其更切合实际。本书的写作方法也正是基于这一理路。

为了定义一个对象，我们必须要知道我们必须用它做什么，以及它可以为我们做什么。给一个对象下定义，就是要精确地说明这一对象对我们所表现出的行为或态度。因此，所有所谓真正的知识，就是朝向某一方向或源自某种观点。（Henri Bergson，1934：199）

最初，没有任何事实是具有跨文化性的，跨文化性也不是某一对象的属性，只有通过跨文化的分析，才可以赋予对象这一属性。（Martine Abdallah-Pretceille，2006：480）

本书的内容是教育中的跨文化性问题。在此我使用了“interculturality”

一词，而并未将“intercultural”这一形容词作为名词使用，加入“-ality”这一后缀形式表明跨文化是一种过程和正在形成的事物。这一术语与本书中所讨论的教育中的跨文化性最为接近。虽然至今我已就跨文化性的概念以不同语言著书近15年，但在本书开篇我就提出，自己并不确定跨文化性的涵义和其在当今时代的具体指向，也并不确定其内涵和外延的具体所指，当然，这看起来确实有些自相矛盾。我同意上文所提及的两位学者的观点，他们对我的研究工作影响很大：“跨文化性是一种观念，而不是一种既定事实。”这意味着，是我们自己决定了什么是跨文化的，而非他者所定义。这就使得跨文化这一概念变得不稳定，并带有政治和意识形态的色彩。在我的研究中，很多情况下我都试图摆脱这一概念，但并没能找到更好的语词来替代。我只能又回到“跨文化”这个词。身处学者市场化和品牌化愈发成为惯例的学术界，跨文化也便成了我的研究身份的一部分，它像“水蛭一样牢牢附着在我的身体上”。而当我遇到其他跨文化交流和教育领域的研究者和实践者时，“跨文化性”一词常常会使我们产生兄弟般的情谊，并带来许多便利。但令人遗憾的是，我们既不讲同一种语言，对这一概念的理解也不尽相同。“我的跨文化”可能与“你的跨文化”含义不同。“我的跨文化”可能与“你的跨文化”包含不同的价值观和意识形态。本书尝试帮助人们认识到跨文化性这一概念，并分享笔者在过去的十年中与来自世界各地的同事和学生对跨文化性的意义和研究方法的讨论。

让我从一个老生常谈的话题开始：跨文化自古以来就与我们同在。人们总是跨越各种界线去交流。例如，跨越不同国家、地域、语言、宗教和/或社会（Pieterse，2004）等。因此，与我们现在认为的不同，跨文化性并不是一个全新的现象。而当下与过去的差别在于：当下，跨文化现象是无处不在的，而且它发生的速度更快。然而，“我们的”跨文化可能并不比过去更好。即使我们认为，我们目前的跨文化交流和互动正在快速增长，但很明显，我们这个飞速发展的世界与McLuhan所描述的“地球村”并不相同。在“地球村”中，信息、物品和人类的运动都是即时的，进而产生更多的接触和互动（Wolton，2013：163）。与此同时，教育大概是学习、练习和反思跨文化性的最佳途径，当然，我们也很少有时间在其他领域中体悟跨文化性。众所周知，跨文化既是学校生活的一部分（多元化的学生），也是教与学必不可少的组成部分（学校中所有科目或明显或含蓄地都提到了跨文化交际）。在一个种族主义、歧视和不公都在加剧的世界里，学校更应为学生成为真正的跨文化者提供有效帮助，让他们能够对这些现象提出怀疑，从而做出有道德意识和批判精神的行动。

跨文化性是教育中很流行的一个概念。但在20世纪60年代以来的美国，20世纪70年代以来的欧洲以及近期世界的其他部分国家和地区，跨文化性常与多元文化主义、文化跨越性、社会公平或全球化等概念相混淆。像教育中其他许多重要概念一样，跨文化性往往是多义的、虚构的，同时又是空洞的，人们常常会夸大或缩小这一概念的意义。笔者还记得，有一天看到了英国广播公司（BBC）热播电视剧《滑铁卢大道》（*Waterloo Road*，2006—2014）中的一个场景，该剧剧情发生于一所名为“滑铁卢大道”的综合学校中。在那个场景中，学生发展部主任正在为当地教育部门的来访准备手册。她与学校校长共同编写了以下内容：

学生发展部主任：…… 向社会证明，社区是我们“滑铁卢大道”学校的一部分，而学校同时也是社区的一部分 ……（对校长说话）这些行话您觉得够了吗?

校长：我想还可以大量加入您的多元文化专业知识。

学生发展部主任：好的。您看这个怎么样？坎贝尔小姐，她将回答有关学校种族多样性的问题……我们所采取的措施是为了确保每个孩子，不论他们的种族、宗教或文化，都能得到平等和尊重。

“行话”和“大量加入”这两个词可以很容易地用来描述教育中跨文化（性）的有关研究和实施状况。

跨文化性的核心是跨学科，同时也通过借鉴其他研究领域的理念、概念和方法构建。此外，教育中的跨文化实践和研究范式深受国家政策和意识形态的影响，而这些政策和意识形态并不总是与跨学科的讨论或现实相一致。因此，借用马基雅维里（Machiavelli）的区分，我经常有这样一种印象，“宫殿式的思考”（学者、决策者、教育家）远胜过“公共广场式的思考”（体验跨文化经历的人；Maffesoli，1985：184）。换句话说，当涉及跨文化交流时，强者往往会强势地代替弱者说话，甚至会盖过弱者的声音。最后，在研究和实践中，这一概念被应用于许多不同的领域，如应用语言学、语言教育、传播学、教育、卫生等。因此，当这一概念在各个领域、子领域和机构中传播时，它的意义有时得以保留，有时则会被修改，有时甚至会成为灌输和传播刻板印象、偏见和偏差的混合体。

本书的方法

本书提出了一种方法，即以批判和反思的立场解读教育的跨文化性概念。受A. Holliday的跨文化交流方法（2010）的启发，笔者认为跨文化是经典马克思主义的意识形态，是一种评价性的，而非中性或描述性的概念。因此，跨文化性指的是这样一种权力状态，即一些人被“支配、排斥和歧视”，而另一些人则倾向于通过用“我们”和“他们”这类表述来假装自己公正公平地对待他们（Shi-xu，2001）。

本文提出了以下问题：

—— 当今跨文化的含义是什么？

—— 这一概念的背后暗含了什么样的意识形态？

—— 应如何描述这一概念的特征？

—— 为什么我们需要改变教育中的跨文化实践？

—— 一个人能接受一种新型的跨文化教育和培训吗？

—— 有“良好”实践的案例吗？

本书所提出的跨文化教育方法认为，跨文化（intercultural）的前缀“inter-”（跨）能够对跨文化的含义进行最佳诠释：互动、情境、权力关系的认识、简单复杂性（Simplexity，简单与复杂不可避免的组合）、交错性（Intersectionality，种族、民族、国籍和语言等不同身份如何促进跨文化性）。同时，本书对该概念的第二部分 ——“cultural”（文化）也有修正。

本书就像一个工具箱，通过提出某些概念、见解和方法来评估和重构跨文化性这一概念，使其在研究和实践中更好地发挥作用，同时更加适应这个加速变化的全球化时代（Accelerated globalization）。本书还呼吁应多极考虑教育的跨文化性。本书向读者介绍了截至目前的跨学科观点，这些观点基本组成了跨文化概念。各种研究项目和文化作品的具体案例都阐述了这些“工具”。本书每一章都以自我反思性问题结尾。在本书的最后，笔者列出了十篇与跨文化教育相关的重要的参考文献。本书适用于对跨文化教育、语言教育、传播教育以及教师教育感兴趣的学生、学者（新手和研究人员）以及相关的实践者，相信你们一定会有所收获。

参考文献

ABDALLAH-PRETCEILLE，M. Interculturalism as a paradigm for thinking about diversity [J]. Intercultural Education，2006，17（5），475–483.

BERGSON H. The creative mind：An introduction to metaphysics [M]. New York：Kensington Publishing Corp，1934.

HOLLIDAY A. Intercultural communication and ideology [M]. London：Sage，2010.

MAFFESOLI M. La connaissance ordinaire：Précis de sociologie comprehensive [M]. Paris：Librairie des Méridiens，1985.

PIETERSE J. N. Globalization and culture：Global mélange [M]. Lanham：Rowman and Littlefi eld Publishers，2004.

SHI–XU. Critical pedagogy and intercultural communication：Creating discourses of diversity，equality，common goals and rational-moral motivation [J]. Journal of Intercultural Studies，2001，22（3），279–293.

WOLTON D. Le monde n' est pas un village. L' Express [EB/OL]. http：//www.lexpress.fr.libproxy.helsinki.fi/informations/dominique-wolton-le-monde-n-est-pas-un-village_651315.html#TMPXQLFMABUCg8Cl.99.

第二章　用词不当

摘　要：本章讨论并修正了三个经常与跨文化紧密联系且有问题的概念。这三个概念分别是文化、身份和集体。文化这一概念一直是跨文化研究和实践的中心。然而，许多研究领域常常会质疑文化这一概念过于固化和泛化。因此，本章提出了一种流动性的概念。同样，身份这一概念是当今时代的中心概念，对理解跨文化概念非常重要。笔者认为，我们需要从共同建构主义的立场来对身份进行审视。最后，笔者通过结合后现代的跨文化性，也对集体这一概念进行了重新定义。

> 最好是做东西文化的比较。这是当今一个时髦的话题，不管你写的是什么（不是什么）都不重要，只要你坚定自己的说法，就能推销出去。（老舍，1929：75）

跨文化自20世纪50年代在交流领域和20世纪70年代在教育领域提出以来，这一概念一直在全球各地广泛传播。Blommaert所说的“旅行话语”（2005：72）就是关于跨文化传播的一个很好的例子。对于学者们来说，当此一话语在全球范围内“旅行”时，只能体现出话语的外形，而话语的内在价值、意义或功能却无法进行真正的“旅行”。跨文化研究需要使用某些特定历史背景下的概念——这就需要了解这些话语的不同含义和其背后的相关的意识形态。在这一节中，笔者回顾了人们在研究教育的跨文化问题时，颇具争议但仍被大量使用的一些概念。需要指出的是，它们实际上是一种用词不当（对一个术语的错误或不准确的使用），也就是说，它们引发并导致了对一些不可靠、甚至是不真实的跨文化现象的解释。当然，人们需要意识到，在跨学科讨论时，才能质疑这些解释。本节还警示读者存在一种危险性，即在探讨跨文化性时，把它当作概念去做事和思考，而不是人在做事和思考。拟人主义（Anthropomorphism）的思想，或者将人类的特性赋予除人类之外的存在、物体和概念，反映出一种将文化、社区和多样性等概念个人化的倾向，使它们以某种方式去做事和思考，而不是人去做事和思考。换句话说，人消失在这些概念中。一些短语就是很好的例子，比如“与其他文化的沟通”“文化遇见文化”“与穆斯林社区的交流”等等（上述有问题的用法见于Bender-Szymanski，2013）。跨文化教学法中此类用法也很普遍，比如“融入外国文化的意愿”和“基于考虑和个人情况批判性地融入外国文化”。我的问题是：在这些话语表达中，人在哪里？是谁通过这些拟人化的语言来替他们说话？

“看似舒适的文化温床”（ERIKSEN，2001）

几年前，我在一次全球大学峰会（Global University Summit）上目睹了一件非常有趣的事情。来自世界各地的数百名学生聚集在一起，商讨针对海外留学的建议，以期为二十国集团（G20）下次会议提供参考。二十国集团峰会是一个由世界20个主要经济体的政府和中央银行行长所召开的国际论坛。一篇由会议组织者撰写的文章成了本次会议展开讨论的基础。学生们围绕“文化”和“文化冲击”两个概念展开了有趣的讨论。学生明显分为两个阵营：一部分学生拒绝将“文化冲击”一词用于解释国际学生在国外遇到问题的原因，同时，“文化冲击”也不应成为政府向国际学生提供帮助的理由，因为这一词语不仅语义模糊，而且过度依赖于“文化”一词；另一些学生则认为“文化冲击”是一个具体现象，他们在“其他文化”中曾遭遇过“文化冲击”。我支持那些对这些概念的价值持怀疑态度的人，因为这些概念太过“舒适”了。

文化这一概念在“跨文化”一词中处于中心地位，但我们应该如何对待它呢?

文化一直是跨文化教育讨论的重点。然而，自20世纪80年代以来，许多领域中出现了一个关键转折，导致文化的概念及使用方式被修订，或是直接遭到抛弃。人类学就是其中的领域之一，这一领域曾经严重依赖于文化的概念（Starn，2015）。本节内容中，针对文化，我们呼吁一种方法，即能够超越虚无缥缈的固化的民族文化概念并讨论这一概念的本体论方面的问题（这将文化变为一个“借口”）。

文化和其概念并不存在必然联系。这句话就像对用词不当念咒语一样，将贯穿整节内容。文化和其概念不是代理关系；它们不是轻易能互相感知的。一个人不可能遇到一种文化，但却可以遇到代表文化的人——或者说是代表了文化想象和特征的人。Wikan（2002：83）表达了她对“人们说话的倾向，好像文化被赋予了心智、情感和意图”的惊讶。……好像文化有了自己的生命”。Phillips（2007：45）提醒我们，文化既没有界限，也不是封闭的；它并不是同质的；它是“由人产生，而不是解释他们行为方式的存在”。

这就是为什么所有的文化习惯，以及所有所谓的文化遗产，都是与其“文化”的代表者接触和融合的结果。试图定义文化或文化界限，往往会导致封闭和隔离，把它从一个与之互动并影响它的世界中分离出来。有一个关于中国的案例。伦敦大英博物馆的何鸿卿爵士展厅（Joseph E. Hotung Gallery）展示了旧石器时代至今来自中国、南亚和东南亚的文物。在展示中国文明的展区，人们发现了12个五颜六色、令人印象深刻的陶瓷人俑，它们出土于公元700年唐代著名军事家和政治家刘廷荀将军的坟墓。众所周知，公元700年的唐朝，“无论对国内还是国外，都是一个黄金时代”（Mac Gregor，2010：55）。那是丝绸之路的全盛时期。这些造像，包括人类和动物，大约有一米高，排列整齐，是为了保护墓主人，并给地下世界的审判者留下深刻印象，使得地下世界的审判者“承认墓主人的地位和能力，并赋予他在死后世界中应有的地位”（Mac Gregor，2010：55）。对于未经训练和一无所知的人来说，这些雕塑看起来非常“中国”，甚至是“典型的中国脸”。然而如果当一个人凑近去看广目天王（世界的守卫者）塑像的脸时，他就会看到一张印度人的脸。队伍的后面是马和骆驼，这些马是当时中国的新品种，它们来自于西方国家，而双峰驼则来自阿富汗和土耳其斯坦。上文提到印度、阿富汗和土耳其斯坦时，事实上都强调了中国与中亚以及世界其他地区的紧密联系。像其他国家一样，中国一直与世界保持联系，中国文化不仅经历了各种不同文化的多次融合（Mélange），同时也经历了不同时代的变迁与创新。像刘廷荀墓这样的文化产物也象征着“他者”的符号权力，以及“文化”之间的权力关系。因此，从世界其他地方“引进”并货币化了的马和骆驼，有助于这位将军在面对地下社会的审判者时，仍享有崇高的地位。

一些学者也批评了文化概念的使用，因为它往往给人一种印象，即文化应该获得那些理应代表它的人的一致认可（Bayart，2005：74）。在这种情况下，人们仍然被禁锢在文化的“紧身衣”中，或者如Prashad所说（2001：ix），文化“将他们包裹在令人窒息的怀抱中”。Adib-Moghaddam（2011：19）提醒我们，一致的文化并不存在，因此，对于文化（或文明）冲突的讨论是非常值得怀疑的（Bayart，2005：103）。人可以产生冲突，但文化不能。

对文化概念最激烈和严肃的批评是关于文化偏见和意识形态的使用。

首先，文化可以用来解释一个群体的习惯、观点、态度等。对于Piller（2011：172）来说，在这方面，“文化有时只不过是一种方便而懒惰的解释。”通常，当一个人无法解释或理解跨文化时，很容易将文化作为借口或托辞（Dervin and Machart，2015）。在下面的摘录中，可以看到一个芬兰人在试图解释为什么芬兰人是沉默寡言的（这是一种刻板印象）：

> 是的，我们可能比其他国家的人更安静。为什么这会是一个大问题？它只是芬兰文化的一部分。这并不意味着我们很沮丧或其他什么，这只是芬兰（人）的习惯而已。

请注意她是如何用芬兰文化来为芬兰人的习惯和态度“找借口”和去人为化的——换句话说：不是我们，而是我们的文化。Baumann（1996：1）在对英国希思罗机场附近的绍索尔小镇居民的研究中指出了同样的问题：

> 无论任何“亚裔的”被调查者说了什么或做了什么，报道总是把这些解读为他们的一致的“亚洲性”“种族身份”或他们“社区”的“文化”。其他所有因素似乎都缺席了，文化成为被禁锢的蚕茧，或是决定性的力量。

上述芬兰人与Baumann研究中的“亚洲人”的区别在于，芬兰人自己对芬兰文化做了概括，而“亚洲人”则被禁锢于别人所创造的文化当中。

在跨文化交际中，文化的“力量”也被用来解释人们为什么会不理解或误解对方。这一假设是：人们有文化背景（的）不同，所以当他们相遇时，就会产生问题。Sarangi（1994：418）却提出质疑，为什么文化背景不同时会被贴上“跨文化误解”的标签，而“‘文化’背景相同的人遇到问题时，就只被叫作一种挑战”。在许多来自不同国家的人产生误解的例子中，跨文化性实际上与文化无关。

其次，为了描述我们自己的文化，我们需要把它与其他文化进行比较。虽然这被认为是“正常”和/或“自然而然”的，但不难发现其中将会产生的问题（Holliday，2010：39）。这样的比较会产生“好”和“坏”、“文明”和“不文明”、“相同”和“其他”的二分法，进而导致民族中心主义（Ethnocentrism，认为我们的文化比其他文化更好）、权力失衡、高人一等、闭门造车、隐藏或为负面行为辩护（如攻击言论自由、侵犯人权、贬抑女性等等）等。进行文化比较还会造成“包法利主义”（Bovarysm）态势（指法国作家福楼拜小说中的一位女士，她不满意目前的生活，欺骗她的丈夫，入不敷出），即一个人“高看自己，歪曲自己对他人和事物的看法来满足自己扭曲的意志”（Jenson，2006：167）。接下来我将回顾三个关于上述现象的例子，都是在教育的跨文化中需要避免的。

第一个例子，在芬兰人的想象中，芬兰人有一种特殊的文化特征，他们声称这是他们独一无二的 —— sisu。虽然很多人认为这个词无法翻译成其他语言，但英语中的终极决心（ultimate determination）、坚韧（fortitude）和坚持（persistence）几个词都很好地解释了sisu的意义。事实上，sisu一词的来源并不久远：它是在第二次世界大战期间发明的，以此用来激励芬兰军队。我们芬兰人坚韧不拔、意志坚定，在精神上和情感上都很坚强，足以面对困难、逆境和危险。时至今日，这个词仍在日常对话、政治活动以及国家品牌推广和市场营销中被使用，乃至过度使用甚至是滥用。虽然我们需要尊重成千上万在战争中战斗过的人，因为对于他们来说，sisu这个词可能是意义非凡的，但是它在当今社会的使用令人咋舌，特别是当它被用来比较“我们”芬兰人和“其他人”时。这种比较总会无一例外地导致民族中心主义和道德审判。我们比你们更顽强，更勇敢。有趣的是，很少有人注意到sisu与被滥用的口号“Keep calm and carry on”（保持冷静，继续前进）之间的相似之处，这是英国政府在1939年为提高英国公众备战的士气而发明的口号。“Keep calm and carry on”与sisu具有相同的意义 —— 这表示，芬兰的sisu并非独一无二的。

第二个例子来自一本小册子，几年前这本小册子主要用以分发给芬兰一所大学的国际学生。这本小册子是为了教导这些学生如何在学校“遵规守纪”（Dervin和Layne，2013）。在接下来的摘录中，这本册子的编者向学生们说明了学校对学生在自主性方面的期望：

在许多文化中，学生应该听从老师和导师的指示，而芬兰人鼓励学生独立解决问题，并在必要时采取主动。因此，尽管在许多文

> 化中，年轻人生活在一种被保护、被监督的生活中，但是芬兰的学生非常独立，他们对自己的学习负责。这一点常常使外国学生感到困惑。

值得注意的是，通过使用文化的概念，这本手册的编者得以将：（1）芬兰人和芬兰文化定位为优秀者和优秀文化；（2）将其他文化贬为低一等的文化。同样值得注意的是，此段文化论述中的人，从“在许多文化中的人”和“在许多文化中的年轻人”到“外国学生”，都统归为后者的能力——在此案例中，后者的能力即为无能。这种关于“我们的”文化和“他们的”文化的论述显然是非常有偏见的，同时带有意识形态的色彩，根本不会导向跨文化性。我恰恰认为，“跨”（inter-）的潜在创造性被一种可鄙的教育文化方法所吞噬了。

第三个也是最后一个例子发生在西班牙，一位文化专家花了几天时间探问西班牙人对“文化”的看法。令她惊讶的是，西班牙人似乎并不像她想象的那样，在午餐后午睡。以下是她根据自己的观察做出的解释：

> 据我所知，西班牙人每天大概7点钟下班，如果他们有孩子在家的话，就给孩子吃一些零食，之后傍晚餐厅开门后吃一些塔帕斯风味小吃，然后再匆匆忙忙到晚上12点或者1点。所以在我看来，他们每晚平均睡眠只有5到6个小时，我真的不知道这是为什么？尤其因为我来自瑞典，我们瑞典人需要非常多的睡眠。是因为气候吗？还是因为即使在西班牙人们也得更加努力地工作？

我着重强调了“即使”这一副词，因为它揭示了这位顾问的主观性和对西班牙人及其文化的一种含蓄的消极看法。在“即使”一词背后隐藏的是，（她）认为西班牙人懒惰这一令人厌恶的刻板印象。有趣的是，通过她在开头描述的非常普遍和“机器人般”的日程安排，她也在试图质疑西班牙人过得很轻松这一假设。

Hoskins和Sallah（2011：114）已经证明了文化这个词的某些用法——正如上面摘录的那样——常常会导致仇外心理（Xenophobia，对外国人和陌生事物的恐惧）、种族主义、性别歧视、身份简化，甚至是某些形式的身体暴力和符号暴力（Sen，2005）。

那么我们该如何处理文化的概念呢？如果没有文化，我们能处理好教育中的跨文化现象吗？许多学者认为，我们需要保留文化的概念（Ogay和Edelmann，2011），避免“把婴儿随洗澡水一起倒掉”。在我个人的研究中，我选择把“婴儿”倒掉，因为它对学生、研究人员、从业者和决策者带来了太多的困惑和误解。我与我的对话者对于文化的理解常常是不一样的。我拒绝用一个将“他者”从个人的多元环境中摒弃的词语，所以也避免使用这个空洞且会带来问题的概念。所以，如果没有“文化”这一核心概念，我们应该怎么办呢？ Eriksen对此提出了非常有用的建议：

> 如果一个人谈论本地艺术，他可以直接说“本地艺术”，而不用将文化牵扯其中；如果一个人谈论语言、意识形态、父权制、儿童权利、饮食习惯、宗教仪式或地方政治结构，他可以直接使用这些词或是类似的术语。（Eriksen，2001：141）

同理而言，Wikan（2002：86）建议使用“知识”“经验”或“生活世界”这三个词。只有在使用文化等特定词汇时表达得越精准和清晰，我们才能更好、更加公平地处理教育的跨文化性的问题。

身份不是恒定物

本节回顾了跨文化讨论中身份概念的含义。与文化的概念不同，我相信如果我们使用一个开放的、过程性的、共同建构的方法，那么身份对于检验跨文化问题会非常有用。

教育往往使人相信，我们的身份是恒定不变的。然而与此同时，当我们遇到其他人时，我们会经历什么往往是变幻无常、不可预测的（Lifton，1993）。这就是为什么我们有时决定躲在面具后面，或者把对方简化成某一个身份。我们都有不同的身份，这些身份取决于语境和对话者，也取决于我们的健康、心情、说话意愿等。A.Sen（2005：350）也提醒我们：

> 一个人可以生于印度，是一个帕西人，同时也是一个法国公民，一个美国居民，一个女人，一个诗人，一个素食主义者，一个人类学家，一名大学教授，一个基督徒，一个鸟类观察家，一个狂热的外星生命信徒，她相信外星生物会乘着五彩缤纷的不明飞行物在宇宙中翱翔。

所以，从某种意义上说，根据Turkle（1996）的理论，当我反思自己时，与其问“我是谁?”，不如问“我们是谁?”更合适。更准确地说，这个问题应该是“对于其他人来说，我们是谁?”因为正是通过他人的眼睛，我的自我才得以建立，我的身份才得以存在。当然有的事情并不总是那么顺利。事实上，虽然有些人可能觉得自己可以自由地使用他们的多重身份，有些人却可能会被限制在固定而单一的身份上，就像被装填固定为展品或标本的动物皮毛一样（Chebel d' Appollonia，2011：11）。许多情况下，是我们自己希望将身份减少为一个固定的身份（Baumann，2004），因为我们可能觉得在特定环境下向他人公开自己的某些身份，并不是件愉快的事（比如种族、性取向等）。

许多研究跨文化的学者认为，我们应该意识到自己的身份，并/或学会为自己是谁而感到骄傲（例如Byram，1997）。我相信这是一种幻觉，因为我是谁不是恒定不变的，它会根据不同环境而变化，并且也是同他人协商的结果。事实上，如果一个人开始在身份中寻找恒定不变之处，他将面临许多挑战：我们对过去的记忆会变，记忆也与其他人不同；我们可以获得新的国籍，摆脱旧国籍；在许多国家改名字也不是一件难事；整形手术和化妆品也可以或多或少改变我们的外貌。出生日期可能是我们唯一不变的身份标记。但是有些情况下，人们可以要求政府有关部门更正他们在官方文件上的出生日期。尽管令人惊讶，但有些人可能连自己真正的出生日期都不知道，或使用了错误的日期。以下案例是一位女士在网上分享的：

> 我真正的出生日期是1998年3月10日，但是我父母给我的出生证明上显示我的生日是1997年4月4日。由于这个原因，我所有的证件，比如学校的毕业证书和护照上的生日都是错的。我能不能把我的生日改成我真正的生日？求助！（匿名，日期已变更）

对于作家Hanif Kureishi（1998：n. p.）来说，试图寻找身份是徒劳的。

他解释说：

> 我想，当你意识到没有所谓的“身份”时，你的问题就解决了，因为在某种意义上，这个问题对你来说已经不存在了。当我还是个住在郊区的年轻人时，我走在街头遇到人问我，你从哪里来？我说从那边的房子来。他们会说是的，但是你到底是从哪里来的？这真的会让我感觉很困扰，因为我真的是从那边的房子里出来的，除此之外，我不知道该说什么。当然，我的父亲是印度人……你如何将不同的自我概念组合在一起，从而形成通常所说的自我（我的转录）。

对于那些看起来与“大多数人”（不同肤色、外国口音）不同的人来说，他们是谁的问题可能会经常成为与他人讨论的话题。“你来自哪里？你真正来自哪里？你听起来像外国人，你是哪国人？”尽管这些问题在跨文化交流中似乎是“正常的”，但问这些问题可能会带有政治意味，回答起来也让人觉得非常困难且令人烦恼，十分尴尬。在我们的社会中，有人总需要解释他们的身份，而有人则不需要。有时他们不得不面对这种类似警察调查的局面。在教育领域中，我们需要特别注意这一点。有时我们觉得把别人的出身摆到桌面上是一件好事，这样可以讨好他们或是给予他们更多权力。然而，我们对对方的假设可能会伤害到他人。这倒不是因为拥有不同肤色或种族的人有不同国籍或语言。恰恰是因为我在芬兰目睹过许多荒谬的情况。一位出生在芬兰的亚裔，在商店必须努力跟店员说芬兰语。因为店员用英语和她说话，完全忽略了她会说芬兰语这一事实。另一种情况是，一位英语老师正在用英语教不同水果的名字，然后她转向班上的一个黑人学生，用英语问她非洲人吃什么水果。这个学生很尴尬，只能回答说她出生在芬兰，从来没有去过非洲，也对那里吃的水果一无所知。在下一章中，我们将通过“变自我为他者”的工具来讨论这一现象。

国家、文化和群体身份常常是跨文化讨论的中心。对于许多思想家和研究人员来说，这些都是有问题的。首先，它们往往会造成出于政治动机的人为分化，并会导致歧视、民族中心主义和毒害。其次，Pieterse（2004：33）解释道：

> 国家身份是一种融合（Mélange）的身份，是按照惯例被合并在一个政治标题下的人的组合（如凯尔特人、法兰克人和其他“法国”人）。

正如我在前一部分提到的，教育中应优先理清这种混合身份。这些身份既不是“天生的”，也不是“上帝赋予的”（Said，1993：33），它们代表了一种“分析型刻板印象”（analytical stereotypes；Sarangi，1994），因为它们迫使我们在那些实际上可能有很多共同点的人之间建立明确的界限。我们也要记住，我们已经进入了这样一个身份市场化的时代。国家品牌化（National branding）是常见的全球现象，政府借此决定什么是本国的象征，什么可以作为周边产品进行出售，以及如何从中牟取暴利（Comaroff和Comaroff，2009）。这些身份形成的经济维度（Halter，2000：12）创造了新形式的民族主义和民族中心主义，我们需要在教育中对这一形式进行反击。2015年11月的一则新闻，解释了一位法国艺术家如何根据其画廊的要求，为自己创造中国身份后打入中国市场，甚至间接打入国际市场。由此，他的作品开始卖得比用他真名时好得多。他的画廊曾表示，国际艺术品投资者更愿意投资一位在中国拥有中文名字的艺术家。结束本节之前，让我们看看米歇尔·福柯（1982：10）提出的一个明智的建议：

> 我觉得没有必要确切地知道我是什么。最有趣的是在生活和工作中成为你一开始就没有成为的那个人。如果当你开始写一本书时就知道结尾要说什么，你认为你还会有勇气写它吗？

不知道对方是谁——尤其是在关乎带有偏见和问题的身份，如文化、国家身份时——可以改变我们跨文化的方式，重新平衡权力关系，带来更加原汁原味的交际。就像香港喜剧演员、电影导演李力持对“你是香港人还是中国人?”的回答，我们也可以更多地把自己和他人视为“地球人”（《香港杂志》，2015：42）。

集体、自我和他者

> 问题还在于，“集体”这个词是用来描述一个人发自内心自愿加入的集体感，还是仅靠同样的民族身份而产生的集体统一感这种刻板印象。（Baumann《关于社区》，1996：15）

在跨文化交流中，集体可以发挥重要作用。它可以帮助我们强化自己的身份，让我们自我感觉良好，将自己和他人区分开来。如前所述，身份是通过与他人的互动产生的，他人（不得不）代表了其他群体、其他社区。在这一部分中，我感兴趣的是“社区”（community）一词的使用以及它与跨文化的联系。

尽管越来越多的学者对“社区”一词的使用持批评态度，但它在今天仍是一个时髦的词语。它经常被描述成一个非常模糊的术语：“社区从来就不是一个词法精确的术语，尽管有大量枯燥的研究想要描绘这一词语的概念，但仍然一无所获。”（Cohen，2002：165）这一概念也在很多不同领域被讨论过，如社会学、人类学、社会心理学和心理学（Anderson，1983；Cohen，1985；Maffesoli，1996；Bauman，2001；Amit，2002；Brubaker，2007；Auge，2010）。在日常话语或研究论述中，其他概念也经常与社区交替使用，这些概念也因其对人的“作用”而受到批评，比如“群体”（group）一词。Rogers Brubaker（2007：7）认为，“群体”是一个看似没有问题、理所当然的概念，显然不需要特别的审视或解释。然而，Gerd Baumann（1996）已经证明，在欧洲，“社区”和“群体”往往被用来指代“其他”，即“非西方”的人群。在跨文化语境中，人们常常会谈论穆斯林社区、亚洲社区、俄罗斯社区等等，但很少会谈论法国社区或西班牙社区。这些社区中包括谁或不包括谁却从没明确过。此外，谁有权利为这些社区发声也是个问题。

许多学者为解码当今的集体概念提供了替代词语，比如“新部落”（neo-tribes）、“存在集合”（etre-ensemble；Maffesoli，1996）和“夹子社区”（peg-communities；Baunman，2004）。Maffesoli或Baunman对我们这个时代的分析显示，具有意义的新社区正在变得清晰可辨。Bauman（2004：31）将“夹子社区”定义为“短时间内将个人的关注点挂在一个共同的‘夹子’上所形成的社区”。类似地，Maffesoli（1996：75）认为，“新部落主义的兴起和繁荣”与这样一个事实有关：人类群体“拒绝认同任何政治项目，拒绝接受任何一种终局”。他补充说，群体成员在一起

“唯一的原因是习惯了集体的存在”。社会学家给出了其所称为的“情感部落”（Maffesoli，1996：75）的例子，即基于（短期的）情感依恋形成的有组织或无组织的群体，比如试图“复兴”“遗产”的宗教、语言和“民族”群体；比如体育、音乐、节日活动；比如表达公众团结和慷慨的活动；比如体育俱乐部、办公室伙伴、粉丝和业余爱好者（1993：13 — 14）。尽管Maffesoli首先将“新部落”定义为非政治性的，但在其《我们脑中的危机》（*La crise est dans nos têtes*，2011）一书中，他谈到了2010 — 2011年反对资本主义的“占领”抗议（纽约“占领华尔街”事件、西班牙“愤怒”事件以及香港地区抗议事件）。Facebook和Twitter等社交媒体也代表了“情感部落”的例子，它们的用户从一个网站导航到另一个网站，并在这个过程中与他人产生共鸣（Coutant和Stenger，2011）。正是通过这些集体，一个人构建了他是谁，并通过这些集体获得幸福和快乐。

社区这一概念经常被反复用于整体主义/集体主义（“非西方的”、传统的）和个人主义（现代的、“西方的”）的二分法中，这种二分法是有缺陷的。这些人为制造的差异会使对方陷入某种人为的独特性当中，并将他/她“冻结”在一种“永久的他者性”状态中（Levinas，1969）。这显然是很有问题的。例如，Emmanuel Lozerand（2010）对日本历史的研究表明，日本的个人主义和欧洲一样常见。Adrian Holliday（2010）在他对跨文化交际中的意识形态的批判性评论中，论证了这种二分法的偏见性，并且缺乏自主性、进步性和现代性（Modernity）。这个中国学生不如我们的学生自主。他太依赖别人了。我们这个时代有一个迷思，就是“西方人”已经抛弃了集体主义，而东方却仍然非常依赖集体主义。而集体主义，即集体对社会存在的影响，同样也是西方社会性的基础。无论愿意承认与否，每个人都与其他群体有关。值得注意的是，当下西方流行的教育学理论都对合作建构主义有很高评价，认为与他人共商共建、共同学习是有效教育的必要条件。

问题

1. 请你周围的人给跨文化中的“文化”一词下个定义。他们的定义有什么共同之处和不同之处？

2. 在一天的课程中，仔细聆听人们在谈论他人（难民、移民、少数民族）时是如何使用文化这个词的。这告诉我们他们对其他人的什么看法？“文化”一词起了什么作用？

3. 和你认识的来自国外或有外国血统的人交谈。问他们对自己的感觉，比如他们觉得自己是芬兰人多一些，还是中国人多一些。仔细听他们的回答，问题本身告诉了我们什么？

4. 想想你自己的身份。你是否相信它的某些元素永远都是一样的？你是否意识到这样一个事实：有时你会让自己适应与你谈话的人或特定的环境吗？

5. 你能清楚地确认你属于多少个群体吗？你能界定这些群体之间的界限吗？这些群体对你的观点、行为和态度有什么影响？

参考文献

ADIB-MOGHADDAM A. A metahistory of the cash of civilisations：Us and them beyond orientalism [M]. New York：Columbia University Press，2011.

AMIT V.（Ed.）. Realizing community. Concepts，social relationships and sentiments [M]. London：Routledge，2002.

ANDERSON B. Imagined communities: Refl ections on the origin and spread of nationalism [M]. London: Verso, 1983.

AUGÉ M. La communauté illusoire . Paris: Payot, 2010.

BAUMAN Z. Liquid modernity [M]. Cambridge: Polity Press, 2001.

BAUMAN Z. Identity . Cambridge: Polity Press.

BAUMANN G. Contesting culture: Discourses of identity in multi-ethnic London [M]. Cambridge: Cambridge University Press, 1996.

BAYART J. P. The illusion of cultural identity [M]. London: Hurst & Co, 2005.

BENDER-SZYMANSKI D. Argumentation integrity in intercultural education: A teaching project about a religious-ideological dialogue as challenge for school [J]. Intercultural Education, 2013, 24(6), 573–591.

BLOMMAERT J. Discourse . Cambridge: Cambridge University Press, 2005.

BRUBAKER R. Ethnicity without groups . Harvard: Harvard University Press, 2007.

BYRAM M. Teaching and assessing intercultural communicative competence [M]. Clevedon: Multilingual Matters, 1997.

CHEBEL D' APPOLLONIA A. Les frontières du racisme [M]. Paris: Presses de Sciences Po, 2011.

COHEN A. The symbolic construction of community [M]. Great Britain: Ellis Horwood, 1985.

COHEN A. Epilogue [M]// V. AMIT (Ed.). Realizing community. Concepts, social relationships and sentiments. London: Routledge, 2002.

COMAROFF J. L. & COMAROFF J. Ethnicity, inc [M] . Chicago: The University of Chicago Press, 2009.

COUTANT A. & STENGER T. (Eds.) . Ces réseaux numériques dits sociaux [J]. Special issue of Hermès, 2011 (59).

DERVIN F. & LAYNE H. A guide to interculturality for international and exchange students: An example of hostipitality ? [J] Journal of Multicultural Discourses, 2013, 8 (1) , 1–19.

DERVIN F. & MACHART R. (Eds.) . Cultural essentialism in intercultural encounters [M]. London: Palgrave, 2015.

ERIKSEN T. H. Between universalism and relativism: "A critique of the UNESCO concept of culture" [M]// J. K. COWAN M. B. DEMBOUR & R. A. WILSON (Eds.) . Culture and rights: Anthropological perspectives. Cambridge: Cambridge University Press, 2001.

FOUCAULT M. Technologies of the self [M]. London: Tavistock, 1982.

HALTER M. Shopping for identity: The marketing of ethnicity [M]. New York: Schocken Books, 2000.

HOLLIDAY A. Intercultural communication and ideology [M]. London: Sage, 2010.

HONG KONG MAGAZINE. Lee Lik-chi thinks Stephen Chow is hiding [EB/OL]. http: //hk-magazine.com/city-living/article/lee-lik-chi-i-was-criticized-those-yellow-ribbons.

HOSKINS B. & SALLAH M. Developing intercultural competence in Europe: The challenges [J]. Language and Intercultural Communication, 2011, 11 (2) , 113–125.

JENSON D. Bovarysme and exoticism [M]// L. D. KRITZMAN & B. J. REILLY (Eds.) . The Columbia history of twentieth-century French thought. New York: Columbia University Press, 2006.

KUREISHI H. In the psychiatrist' s chair – BBC Radio 4 [EB/OL]. http: //www.bbc. co.uk/programmes/b049xlzx.

LEVINAS E. Totality and infi nity [M]. Pittsburgh: Duquesne University Press, 1969.

LIFTON R. J. The protean self: Human resilience in an age of fragmentation [M]. New York: Basic Books, 1993.

LOZERAND E. La question de l' individu au Japon [M]// P. CORCUFF C. LE BART & F. DE SINGLY (Eds.) . L' individu aujourd' hui, Débats sociologiques et contrepoints philosophiques. Rennes: Presses Universitaires de Rennes, 2010.

MAC GREGOR N. A history of the world in 100 objects [M]. London: Penguin, 2010.

MAFFESOLI M. La contemplation du monde [M]. Paris: le Livre de Poche, 1993.

MAFFESOLI M. The time of the tribes: The decline of individualism in mass society [M]. London: Sage, 1996.

MAFFESOLI M. La crise est dans nos têtes! [M]. Paris: Jacob-Duvernet Eds, 2011.

OGAY T. & EDELMANN D. Penser l' interculturalité: l' incontournable dialectique de la différence [M]// A. LAVANCHY A. GAJARDO & F. DERVIN (Eds.) . Anthropologies de l' interculturalité. Paris: L' Harmattan, 2011.

PHILLIPS A. Multiculturalism without culture [M]. Princeton: Princeton University Press, 2007.

PIETERSE J. N. Globalization and culture: Global mélange [M]. Lanham: Rowman and Littlefi eld Publishers, 2004.

PILLER I. Intercultural communication: A critical introduction [M]. Edinburgh: EUP, 2011.

PRASHAD, V. Everybody was kung fu fi ghting: Afro-Asian connections and the myth of cultural purity [M]. Boston: Beacon, 2001.

SAID E. Representations of the intellectual [M]. New York: Vintage Books, 1993.

SARANGI S. Intercultural or not? Beyond celebration of cultural différences in miscommunication analysis [J]. Pragmatics, 1994, 4(3), 409–427.

SEN A. The argumentative Indian [M]. London: Penguin, 2005.

SHE L. Mr Ma and son [M]. London: Penguin Classics, 1929.

STARN O. Writing culture and the life of anthropology [M]. Durham: Duke University Press, 2015.

TURKLE S. The second self: Computers and the human spirit [M]. Boston: The MIT Press, 1996.

第三章　跨文化性的想象

摘　要：跨文化性并不是一种新现象。从古至今它们跨越国界而相遇。在这一章中，作者重新审视了关于跨文化性的各种想象或神话，讨论了全球化、多样性、起源、“相同”和“地方”等概念相关的神话。这些想象已根深蒂固于跨文化性的官方实践和研究话语中，为此，理应寻求跨文化的另类视角，改变我们探讨教育和其他学科中跨文化接触的方式。

与其他当代现象一样，跨文化性是一篇充满想象的记叙文。本节中，我选择了五篇经常会在教育情境中听到的关于跨文化性的神话。而教育中的跨文化的目标之一就应该是讨论和修正这些神话。

首先，我想探讨一下已经被许多学者和思想家讨论过的想象的概念。这些学者都从一个论点开始，即社会性不仅建立在现代理性追求的基础上，同时也建立在想象力的基础上。社会学之父埃米尔・迪尔凯姆（Emile Durkheim，1912 — 1995）在其《宗教生活的基本形式》一文中提出，社会的存在得益于符号形式的共享，这使得人们能够形成集体。他还认为（Emile Durkheim，1995），这导致了“集体欢腾”，有利于社会组带的形成。虽然他并没有提到“想象”这个词，但笔者觉得这些形式，尤其是“集体欢腾”与“想象”的概念是一致的。在2010—2019年，想象是全球本土化的（glocal+local），而不是本土化的。

关于想象的定义往往有相似之处。对于Cornelius Castoriadis（1987）来说，想象有一个统一的共同的核心意涵。同样，Charles Taylor（2004）认为想象是广泛共享的内隐认知图式。他将其定义为“人们想象自己社会存在的方式，如何与他人相处，如维系同伴之间的情感，通常会得到满足的期望，以及这些期望背后潜藏的更深层次的规范概念和形象”（Charles Taylor，2004：32）。精神分析学家Jacques Lacan（1977）给想象增加了一个有趣的维度：他将其视为一种为了满足心理需求而创造的幻想。因此，虽然想象往往是“有条件的”“结构离散的”，或是像有些学者认为的那样，是社区成员间产生认同和互相包容的“模版”（González-Vélez，2002：349），但对另一些人来说，想象代表着“基石活动”的矛盾体，也就是说，想象的背景是不断变化的（Maffesoli，1993）。Salazar（2012：865）认为，对想象的概念化是定义想象最有用的。对于这位人类学家来说，想象是“通过社会传播的具有代表性的组合，这一组合与人们的个人想象相互作用，并被用作创造意义和塑造世界的工具”。因此，想象在自我与他人之间被建构、表达和协商——因此，它们既是稳定的，又是流动的。虽然笔者同意Rivzi（2011：228）的观点，即想象在某些情境下“描述了一种心照不宣的潜意识的社会现象，是由一群人以非反身性的方式来坚持的”，但是人们同样可以对自己的想象具有高度的反身性和批评性。

全球化并不新鲜

这一小节对全球化的概念提出了质疑，并讨论“全球本土化”（glocalization）这一颇有成果的概念。全球化并不新鲜，我们目前所经历的这种全球化直接源于历史进程中的全球化浪潮。Amselle（2001：35）认为，所有社会都是相互影响的（即使他们拒绝）。人们常常把全球化作为我们这个时代的一种特点来谈论。而许多历史学家和人类学家对何谓全球化持不同观点（Subrahmanyam，2011）。J. N. Pieterse（2004）给出了以下例子：

——古代人口在各大洲之间的流动。

——长途、跨文化的贸易。

——“世界宗教”（佛教、基督教和伊斯兰教）。

——技术的传播（军事技术、计算、文学、科学和“新”技术的发明）。

当然，全球化的速度早已今时不同往日，以及它如何系统地对当地造成影响也发生了变化——因此就有了“全球本土化”这个词。它有时被用来代替“全球化”。本地和全球不是完全割裂开来的，而是同一枚硬币的两面。McDowell（1996）用“全球地方主义”（global localism）来指代这一现象。他写道（McDowell，1996：38）：“对所有人来说……无论在地理上是固定的还是流动的，大多数社会关系都发生在当地，发生在一个地方，但一个对思想和信息，对游客和移民，对品味商品和体验食物如此开放的地方是前所未有的。”

S. Huntington（1996）提出的“文明冲突”这一著名观点就因忽视了全球化方面而受到了严厉批评。在《文明的冲突与世界秩序的重塑》一书中，这位政治家认为，文化和宗教将是冷战后冲突的主要根源。在书中，作者把世界划分为排列整齐的文明（西方文明、拉丁美洲文明、东正教文明、东方文明、穆斯林文明等等）。Edward Said 和Amartya Sen等学者对Huntington的著作做出了回应。Said在他2001年的文章《无知的冲突》中解释说，Huntington的理论是荒谬的，因为它没有考虑到不同文化之间的相互依赖和相互作用（Appadurai，2006：164）。在后来的一篇文章中，他甚至指责Huntington是一个种族主义者，是“一个对阿拉伯人和穆斯林实施希特勒政策的拙劣模仿”的支持者。对于Sen（2005）来说，文明冲突的概念是一种危险的认知简化。他解释说：

> 在他的著名著作《文明的冲突》一书中，Samuel Huntington将印度坚定地归为“印度教文明”。通过这种奇特的简化视角，Huntington的观点淡化了印度有更多穆斯林人口的事实（超过1.4亿，比整个英国和法国的人口总和还要多），除了印度尼西亚和巴基斯坦，那些Huntington 口中“伊斯兰文明”国家的穆斯林人口都没有印度的多。可能是基于数字的评估在这里出了什么问题。但是也许使用数据论证的困难恰恰在于论点本身的性质。

我们的世界所经历的不同全球化浪潮导致了资源的不平等和权力的差距（Moghaddam，2008）。当今的世界并无不同，当今的全球本土化在跨文化中扮演了重要角色：有些人比其他人更具符号权力（中心与外围），所以他们说的语言（英语母语者与马来语母语者）、宗教和世界观（新教徒/天主教徒与穆斯林）等也更具符号权力。

对多样性的绝望探索

> 世界是多样的，但这种多样化是不平等的。（De Sousa Santos，2012：241）

过去的十年中，“多样性”这个词在教育中非常流行，被许多“多元兜售家”（diversilogues）、“多元教导家”（diversidacts）和“多元制定家”（diversicrats）所推崇（Wood，2003：16）。多样性甚至已经开始帮助我们构想未来的世界和学校（或是形成对此的想象）。比如在北欧国家，这个词被用来暗指那些与预想的大多数（白人基督徒）不同的种族和宗教。这是一个政治正确的概念，使一些人“好像没有标签，他们就不是人了”（Kureishi，2005）。根据Wood（2003：2）所说，在教育中，多样性指的是“事实”（不同肤色、宗教和语言），但也指希望或愿望。

虽然这一概念只保留给特定的人口阶层（移民、少数族群和宗教少数派），但从一个地方到另一个地方旅行的“精英”代表却被贴上“世界公民”“跨国人员”，甚至是“世界主义者”的标签。可我们什么时候听到过老师给难民儿童贴上“世界主义者”的标签？可能从来没有。为什么有些标签是为某些人保留的？这就要对多样性的概念提出质疑：谁是多样性的？这是什么意思？谁该被贴上标签，谁不该？谁有权决定谁该被贴上标签，谁不该？谁自己有权拒绝被贴上标签？谁决定？多样性（意识形态）这个词背后隐藏的究竟是什么？

Wood（2003：48）已经对这些问题给出了一些答案。多样性这个词经常被用作：

——对一个或多个未命名类别的人的委婉说法。

——总体上是对文化多样性的一种简略说法。

——多样性是把所有能想到的群体识别一遍后剩下的部分。

——文化多样性也可以被用作陈词滥调的浓缩表达。这个陈词滥调是，世界很大，充满了人类的多样性。

就像文化的概念（见第二章）一样，多样性语意如此强大，强大到常常被用来代表人类。我们可能讨论教育中的多样性、课堂多样性对孩子有好处以及课堂多样性的优势等。但是我们在谈论谁呢？根据语境的不同，多样性可以指移民，也可以指难民、穆斯林、非洲人等等。这种多样性往往取决于我们的制度，这些制度决定了他们的外来度/陌生度（等级）、他们的文化和（母）语言。例如，一个孩子的父母出生在台湾，但后来搬到了美国，而他自己出生在美国，但他又可能会因为他的出身被贴上儒家或亚洲人的标签。因此，多样性的思想很容易导致各种有问题的主义，如东西方主义、文化主义（Culturalism）、语言主义、宗教主义，并据此把孩子们分成固定不变的类别。Wood认为，多样性会导致将人“束缚在标签上”。（2003：38）

和Peter Wood（2003）一样，我认为我们通常用来定义教育多样性的方式是人为的、想象的，甚至是捏造的。分享一个日常生活中的例子（你可以轻易在世界各地的学校找到类似的例子）。有一天，我在等回芬兰的航班时，发现自己在一个挤满了“白人”（大部分是芬兰人？）的候机区，大家都已经准备好出示登机牌准备登机。登机区的一面墙上有一大幅艺术作品，描绘了世界各地不同的人们和谐地手拉着手，背景是彩虹和地球。这幅画是一幅典型的多元文化作品，不同“肤色”和“世界观”融合在一起，象征着和平与和谐，这似乎与等候区中白人占多数的场面形成了鲜明对比。这类代表多样性的作品当然不是最近才出现的，早在20世纪90年代，这种多样性就被用在了广告之中。我开始观察我周围的人：这些人群里有不同性别的人，有异性恋、同性恋或双性恋，有富人和穷人，有老人和年轻人，有金色头发的、棕色头发的、紫色头发的，有黑人和白人，有安静的和吵闹的，健康的和不健康的，等等。他们难道不也是多样化的吗？为什么他们的身体没有像来自印度、中国或非洲的人那样在画中被具象化，成为艺术品彰显多样性的标志？为什么在机场这一背景下，肤色、世界观和前面提到的多样性标志之间会存在等级关系呢？这幅机场艺术品和机场现状的对比，以及它仅从种族和宗教的角度错误地展示的多样性，让我们不禁要问几个问题：有多少在候机区的芬兰人想过自己与其他芬兰同胞很相似？他们真的有那么多共同点吗？如果有人说他们只是“正常的”和“典型的”芬兰人，他们会满意吗？他们会投票给一样的政客吗？他们真的有相同的价值观吗？墙上“形形色色”的个人形象同时也具象化了那些等待登机的人……别人是多样化的，而自己不是。

我认为，如果分离多样性群体并对其展开批判，这种等级制度会导致挫折、无知、态度傲慢以及对他人失去兴趣。多样性（Deversity）需要变成多种多样性（Deversities）。这个建议虽然显得离经叛道，却出于以下几个原因。面对某种形式的拒绝和歧视，我们都需要努力去被认可，去建立尊重，（去）反对本质主义（Essentialism），等等。当然，对某些人来说这要容易一些。但在我们这样的时代，即使是处于优势地位的人，由于身份、生活环境变化、疾病等原因，也会致使自己流于劣势地位。我们的责任是共同讨论多种不同形式的多样性，而不是将他们区别开来。我相信这可以帮助我们思想家、研究人员、实践者和决策者同情和认同这些不同（但潜在相似）的多样性。

因此，今天我们对待多样性的方式本身就存在很大的问题和偏见。虽然“多样性”一词应该指多重性，但它却往往意味着差异性和“单一性”。当一方常被禁锢在同质化“多样性”的紧身衣中时，其他大多数人可以自由地宣称自己是“正常的”“不可见的”，因此不需要特别的关注。我同意Wood的观点，多样性（上述概念）是一种系统性的不公平，并使我们成为了不公的帮凶。把人当作物体，好像他们只是他们的种族、阶级、性别和其他肤浅表象的残余，而不是通过他们的思想和创造性行为来定义个体，这是不公平的。举三个例子说明。第一个例子是我在芬兰的一位国际学生观察老师的笔记。她在观摩一节语言课时，老师介绍了表示不同水果的单词：

> 很多水果都是来自异域的，至少对一个北方国家来说是这样。单词表上有很多源自亚洲和非洲的食物：芒果、木瓜等。然后这位老师向一名黑人学生提问，某些水果味道如何，特别是来自她家乡的水果。

作为一名“好”老师，这位教育者想要在课堂上关照到“多样性”的学生，让他们感觉自己是受重视的（她在教师教育中可能学到过这点）。而那名黑人学生却并不走运。她沮丧地告诉老师，她出生在芬兰，从来没有去过非洲，对“那里”的水果一无所知。在此例和其他许多案例中，单独挑出一名学生以显示对学生多样性的关照是老师带有偏见和不公正的行为。另一个借用了Hanif Kureishi（2011：3）的例子，与前一个相似，有一位英国作家，他的父亲来自巴基斯坦。他还记得儿时的这一幕：

> 在我九、十岁的时候，一位老师有意把印度农民在泥棚里的照片放在我面前，并对全班说："Hanif来自印度。"而我在想：我的叔叔们骑骆驼吗？肯定不是穿着西装骑吧？跟我差不多的兄弟们，他们也会半裸着身子，像动画人物小莫格利那样蹲在沙土上，用手吃东西吗？

同样，我假设老师是想通过揭示Hanif的"起源"来为课堂"注入"一些多样性。Kureishi解释说，正是因为这段本质化的插曲，他拒绝自己的印度背景，并为自己与大多数白人不同而感到羞愧难当。

我的最后一个例子也是在教室背景下，取自一本名为《香蕉的生活》的小说（PP Wong，2014）。这里的香蕉指的是一个住在西方的亚洲女孩（白人的内在气质、黄种人的皮肤）。主角出生于英国，她的家庭来自中国。在以下节选中，她谈到了她上学的第一天，以及她的"多样性"是如何出乎意料地被她的老师谈及的（2014：28）：

> 老师：同学们早上！
>
> 同学们：早上好Wilkins老师！
>
> 老师：同学们，在我们开始上课之前，我很高兴向大家介绍一名来自中国的新同学。
>
> （我生于伦敦哈克尼）。
>
> 老师：她的名字叫……

这些例子表明，根据他人的长相做出假设是危险的，将某些人“多样化”的同时也会把班上其他同学当作透明的“机器人”一样对待，也是危险的。本书中所阐释的跨文化性拒绝这种限制多样性的有限方式。我认为多样性与每个人都相关，每位教育者都应该开始从“所有人的多样性”的角度对待每一个人，停止那些捏造的表面化的多样性。我最近在Twitter上看到这样一个描述：“多样性激励了我。”这也应该成为教育的跨文化性的口号——（每个人的）多种多样性激励了我们。

你到底从哪来？

起源问题是教育的跨文化性的核心议题，尽管它也值得商榷。“你来自哪里？”或者“你到底来自哪里？”这样的问题在教育中是无处不在的，特别是当我们与“多样化”的学生打交道的时候。这一部分解释了为什么这类问题可能是过去的事情，以及为什么它可以很容易地创建一个简单的关于“自我”和“他者”之间的故事，并在二者间造成权力的不平衡。Spector（2012）提醒我们，“虽然我们在预测一个人的体能或智力时，很容易因其肤色而产生偏见，但令人惊讶的是，肤色仅由少数基因控制，因此它并不能很好地预测其他25000个基因。事实上，非洲一小块地区的基因多样性比整个欧洲都要多。”

尽管据说我们的世界是后现代的（Postmodernity），即每个人具有多重身份的时代、全球化和世界性的，起源的观念似乎有时对所有人都很重要，有时候却是对无权无势的人最为重要。让我从一件轶事开始。笔者在芬兰组织了一场跨文化交流教育的暑期学校项目，开学时，我解释说，按照我的习惯，我不会让每个学生介绍自己，也不会让他们告诉大家自己来自哪里以及他们的兴趣爱好，等等。我更喜欢他们在课堂活动或喝咖啡或茶的时候，以一种不那么正式、不那么单调乏味的方式相互了解。我介绍了我的研究，但对自己的生活则只字未提，比如我出生的地方（我的“起源”）、我生活和工作的地方、我会说的语言等等。第一节课快结束时，一个学生对我说：“你没有告诉我们你来自哪里，现在你必须告诉我。”在跨文化课程开始时询问讲师他来自哪里似乎很“正常”，也是了解老师的一种方式。但这名学生的语气让我有点恼火（“你必须……”），我回答说，我从哪里来并不重要，我宁愿不说明我的“复杂起源”，因为在接下来长达一个月的课程中，它们肯定会变得显而易见。然后这个学生告诉我他的“种族”和“宗教”身份，并说他为此感到非常自豪。我回答说，他有权利“揭示”他的来源，并为之感到自豪，但我不想在一堂课还有几分钟结束的时候做这样的自我介绍。这名学生很惊讶（可能也很生气）地问我，是否故意要隐瞒我的“起源”，或者我是否为自己的“起源”感到羞耻……通过拒绝阐明我从哪里来，我对福柯（Foucault）的观点（1982）表示了认同：我觉得没有必要知道我是谁。虽然在这种特定的情况下，我做出了这样的反应，但也许在其他情况下，我也会为“揭示”和讨论自己的出身感到自信。例如，当我去理发店的时候，我经常会讨论我到底从哪里来。而这取决于我的心情和所在场所的气氛（人多或少、对理发师的印象等），我可能挑出一个身份放上台面，也可能随便编造一个国籍身份（比如日本），或者就简单回避问题。

“起源”对有些人来说似乎很重要，而对另一些人来说似乎并不重要。在人生的不同阶段，“起源”可能被看作是美好积极、值得夸耀的东西，有时也会变得非常私人、具有政治性、令人苦恼。因此，我们对起源的感觉是相对的，取决于我们的角色、情感、对话者和周遭环境。大多数人在运用起源概念时，把它看作一个显而易见、司空见惯的概念（“我们都有根”），却常常没有意识到起源的问题可能是不稳定的、高度敏感的，并且起源在很大程度上取决于权力。这个词的词源来自拉丁语originem（主格origo），意为“上升、开始、源头”，和词干oriri，意为“上升、变得可见、出现”。起源的观点已经成为全球教育的中心，人“被动”分属于不同的民族国家/种族，这常常被批评为“认知简化”（Sen，2005）和“拟人化概念”，似乎把人当成活生生的肉体，而失却了独立思考和为人处世的能力（agency，Heinich，2009：39）。尽管起源这个词在许多语言中已经存在了多个世纪，并在现代社会中被使用、滥用、过度使用，以决定民族主义的话语和行动中“包含谁”和“不包含谁”，但起源本身是一个非常后现代的主题。因此，即使我们生活在“流动的时代”（Bauman，2004），身份被认为是不稳定、混合和多元的，改变自我的机会也是无限的，但坚持自己的出身或试图寻找自己的起源仍屡见不鲜。许多国家对家谱学重新燃起兴趣，古代语言和传统得到复兴，某人的“遗产”得到发掘等，都有助于重新创造或想象起源，以应对后现代和全球化的压力。根据社会学家Zygmunt Bauman（2004：20）的说法，这些努力与对身份的寻求非常相关，是为了“努力……弥合‘应然’和‘实然’之间的差距”。流动性不仅动摇了国家身份和“想象的社区”（Anderson，1983），同样也动摇了起源。

但我们不能对“起源”完全持否定态度：不可否认的是，无论是国家、社会还是地区，起源都能让人们对自己的身份感觉良好。这就是为什么人们应该有权利按照自己的意愿决定出身——只要不诋毁他人。对于已经移居他乡的人来说，当他们在东道国感到威胁或被边缘化的时候，起源可以作为一种自我安慰的方式。全球化及其可能引发的空虚感和威胁感，都可能会导致人们对起源的渴望。现代性的法律遗留，例如护照，也提升了（好的/坏的）起源的重要性：不是每个人都有能力跨越相同的边界。说一种语言时的不同口音也可以显现一个人的起源，并对他被理解被对待的方式产生影响。这就是为什么有时候，一些移民想要保留或摆脱他们说主流语言时的口音。

一旦人们跨越了边界，起源也能够起到提升"他者"的作用。某些起源被认为比其他起源更好。一些社会——在"东方"和"西方"——为推崇某些起源已经形成了一种积极的歧视：比如一个人可能会由于她的种族、族裔或宗教背景而得到一份工作等等。显性或隐性的积极歧视也可以"提升某些国家和社会主流成员的自我"：从"我们为支持他人做了这么多"到"我们是如此国际化；我们有很多外国人或会说其他语言的人"。由此，起源成了"装点门面的摆设"。起源变得高度政治化。

然而，从另一方面来看，起源可以很容易地满足有效分类的要求，比如出于行政目的，或仅是为了简化研究的复杂性。起源的这种特征导致了这样一个事实，即当今的个体都半推半就地成为了阶序人（Homo Hierarchicus）。Singly（2003：52）提出，与那些不需要讨论、辩护或维护自我起源的人相比，那些"弱势"人群很少有机会去质疑他们的（想象的、预测的、强加的）起源。Singly看到了他称为"起源神话"（2003：58）的危险，因为它很容易产生不合理的等级和比较，而这些会被当权者滥用。他甚至称弱势人群的"起源标签"是极权主义（2003：91）。

就像文化的概念一样，起源可用来为某些实践、行为、态度、话语、意见，甚至价值观提供依据（例如，我来自意大利，这就是我为什么这么做，或者我来自俄罗斯和芬兰之间的卡累利阿共和国，而卡累利阿共和国的人都非常健谈）。许多人类学家和社会学家指出，当人们面对困难（比如喧嚣的战争，Bauman，2004），或是需要通过用如文化、身份、传统、根源、社区等词汇解释他们的所做所想时，起源就有很大可能出现。他们还强调了某些情况下把起源放在第一位的危险性（把人放在“盒子”里），尤其是当起源会导致偏见不公，甚至可怕的政治行为时（Wikan，2002；Sen，2005）。

最后必须记住，每个人的背后都有复杂的经历、故事和起源。这就是这个交叉性概念非常重要的地方。交叉性是指不同的身份标记或不同的种族、性别、社会阶层、年龄等体系的交叉，这种交叉是为了分析起源是如何在教育中“实践”的。如前所述，起源的一个基本特征是不稳定性、可协商性和可变性——换句话说，起源不是静态的。这并不是一个新的观点，但有必要在此重申一下。此外，起源不只是一个（如种族），它们是互相交织、多种多样的。例如，英国伦敦哈罗德百货公司中一位掩面的穆斯林妇女和伦敦西部绍索尔百货公司中一位戴着头巾的妇女是不一样的。不同的门为其而开，她们的遭遇也不尽相同。虽然她们看上去有同样的起源（对于无知的人来说，她们既是阿拉伯人又是穆斯林），但在种族、社会状况、经济地位等方面，她们大概千差万别。

我认为，让人们意识到起源的不稳定性和政治性是很重要的，同样他们必须能够以自己想要的方式协商他们的起源，而不是创造一种起源感。

对于Simmel（2013：39）来说，“教育往往是不完美的，因为所有教育行为都要服务于两股对立的力量：解放和约束”。起源在教育中是无处不在的——无论是社会的、民族的还是文化的。一方面，人们认为起源有助于促进平等、公平和包容。另一方面，Bhatia（2010）认为很多论述，比如关于“少数族群学生”的论述，常常是基于民族主义的教育政策和课程，会导致起源概念的简单化使用，局限了使用范围，导致问题意识的缺失，还很容易导致制度化的种族主义和人群分类。此外，这些也常会有意无意地在人们之间制造等级制度，因为在关于起源、文化和身份的论述背后，有时会隐藏着隐性的道德判断（Holliday，2010）。

当然，我们很容易用一个书面例子来对教师们糟糕的行为（教师在课上无意识地指出学生的起源问题）进行总结概括。许多教育工作者确实试图摆脱这种糟糕的行为。然而根据经验，我们也曾目睹过这种“不好”的行为。需要指出的是，研究人员自己在文章中，也常常以起源的固定指标来开篇（比如国籍或社会阶层），给这些“不好”的行为火上浇油。（鲍曼，2004；Dervin，2011）。我们在探讨研究对象的起源时，大多数时候并没有意识到我们对他们做了什么…… 这就是为什么我相信，就像E. Said（1993：33）所述：

> 说到对于团体或国家身份的共识，学者的任务是表明这些团体不是天生就存在的，也不是上帝创造的，而是一个被构建或制造出来，甚至是被发明出来的实体，其背后隐含着斗争和征服的历史，这些历史有时非常需要去代表。

此外，我认同Singly（2003）的看法，他希望推崇一种“解放”起源的方法：学生应被给予手段和工具来获得起源感，去拒绝/抵制/修正起源感，并在某些情况下能够感觉到自己从被强加的固化的起源中“释放”了出来。笔者还认为，他们应该做好准备回答“你来自哪里?”，这能够将他们从“你为什么在这里?”这一暗含的问题中解放出来。我们不相信，仅靠某个机构或是其中的某位代表，就能决定一个人的起源，还要求被问询者按起源表现自己，就像在学校里一样（见Niemi等人，2014）。

“相同是差劲的”

教育在某种程度上是矛盾的：一方面，它应该帮助学生找到自己的特殊性和个体性（以儿童为中心的方法），但另一方面，教育试图在学生之间创造共性。在这一部分中，笔者分析了处理教育的跨文化性问题时对差异的偏见。虽然学校里经常会赞扬文化差异，但与“他者”的相似性往往会被排斥。这种偏见影响了少数族群学生的待遇，也影响了我们对他们的假设。

我把这种偏执称为差异主义偏见（differentialist bias），或者说是执着地相信人与人之间的不同，而不考虑人们既有不同却也有相同之处的事实。这种偏见常置差异性于跨文化性之上。他者的本质化和市场化，即“异域的”他者（Comaroff和Comaroff，2009），坚持认为他/她是多么的不同。据传2012年，颇具影响力的美国创作型歌手Pharrell Williams为一家日本休闲服装零售商设计了名为“我是另类”（I am OTHER）的时装系列。他的作品之一叫作：“相同是差劲的”，揭示了我在本节所描述的偏见。相关研究和实践也没有对这种适应力极强的群体思维免疫，而是经常收集各种各样的差异性内容来解释或推动教育中的跨文化交流。例如，Harris等人（2011）编写的《文化差异管理》一书中，仅用了12页来论述“跨文化的相似性”。当然，差异很重要，每个人是不同的（在不同文化之间和文化内部），但他们在价值观、想法、行为、观点等方面也可能非常相似。在很多情况下，两个来自不同“文化”的人可能比来自同一个国家的人有更多的共同点。对差异的痴迷似乎与对普遍主义和民族中心主义的恐惧有关。它还会导致在自我中“淹没”他人。

Hannah Arendt（1958：155）在这方面提出了一个重要的观点，她说：“如果人们没有不同，他们彼此之间就没什么可说的了。人们若完全不一样，他们也就不能彼此相互了解。”正如之前所解释的，过度强调文化话语与跨文化的关系，导致研究者和实践者都只考虑到了差异性。对于Jullien（2012：29）来说，差异的概念不够大胆：当我们遇到其他人时，通过观察和（有时）快速讨论，很容易能列出一张差异性表格。这种对他人的态度使我们能够“分配力量、资源和权利”（Hamid，2015：24）。另一方面，如果我们花时间从相似性的视角来审视对方，我们也会开始发现彼此共有的东西、想法和观点。在这层意义上，使用“价值观”一词就会很有意思。笔者经常遇到一些人，他们声称自己（国家）的价值观与他人不同，间接地将自己置于神坛之上。例如：我的文化价值观是诚实、勤奋和民主——这些当然是大多数人共有的价值观。Unni Wikan在她的书（2002：84）中说得很好：

> 谈到“文化”，浮现在我脑海中的画面就是差异、分歧和距离。但说到“人”或“人们”，浮现的画面是一群人为了同样引人注目的大事而奋斗，而有另一群人，尽管存在种种不同，却可以跨越时空与之共鸣。

某些民族更容易被归类到极端不同的相异性中，比如“西方”的中国人（Dervin，2015）。然而，中国也是一个极其多样化的国家，拥有13亿人口，包括各种各样的社会、民族和语言群体。尽管人们拥有共同的护照，但来自伊宁（位于中国西北部的蒙古高原）、齐齐哈尔（位于中国东北部）或南宁（位于中国南部）的学生彼此之间可能没有什么共同点。人们甚至不需要换个城市，就可以在不同的小区或街道遇到各种各样的人，比如在北京。因此，中国人内部是具有多样性的，但与“西方”世界也有共同点。当我和我的团队在北京一所大学的国际学生群体中收集数据时，我们都很高兴听到其中一些人说：“没有像中国人这样的，每个中国人都很不同，每个人都不同，每个城市都不同，所以得看你认识的人是什么样的。有些人很国际化，有些人很传统，你还可以找到更西方化的人。”当然，这句话也有很多值得质疑的地方（如“更西方化”意味着什么？），但这位学生并没有顺嘴说“中国人都是这样的，中国人都是那样的”之类的话。

许多差异主义偏见的“受害者”希望人们能从另一个角度发现他们与其他人的相似之处。在“对多样性的绝望探索”那节中，我所提到的小说《香蕉的生活》（*The Life of a Banana*，2014）中的女孩第一次来学校时，她的英国老师是如何“他者化（Othering）”她的（尽管她在英国出生，但这位老师仍认为“她是中国人”）。在小说中，这个学生也很讨厌被贴上“与众不同”的标签。她说（2014：34）：

> 我开始做白日梦，我想象着在一个没有人认为我与众不同的国家长大会是什么样子。在某个地方，我会很受欢迎，不必解释我的名字或我不是中国人。那将是一个非常酷的地方，在那里亚洲人和牙买加人被视为医生、学生和商人。而不是“中国医生”“亚洲学生”或“年度黑人商人”。在这个国家里，我不会被视为“少数族裔”或“舶来品”，而只被视为“我自己”。那太好了！

这有力地说明了许多教育工作者未能对少数族群学生做的事：不给他们贴标签，不把他们隔离开来。我们生活在一个“正常与不正常、可期待与不可预料、普通与奇异、家养与野生”之间的界限模糊不清的世界，在这些熟悉与陌生中，“我们”与“陌生人”之间的界限也模糊不清（Bauman，1997：25）。这就是为什么，为了创造尊重个性的跨文化实践，我们需要接受那些外表、声音和行为与我们不同的人，实际上可能与我们有许多共同点。

带着批判和反思从相似性而不是差异性出发，可能会为研究和实践开辟新的前景。教育家M. Abdallah-Pretceille（1986）认为，相较于发现差异性，识别相似性可能对提升智商和情商更有益处，因为这需要花费很多时间与人相处并进行深入讨论——而这样的相处和讨论在这个日益繁忙的世界，甚至是在学校中，都是非常缺乏的。

对本土的执着

> 我并不是人们所想的那种人。有次我参加聚会，那里我一个人都不认识。那天在下雨，我淋成了落汤鸡。我提着一个购物袋和一个摩托车头盔。有人错把我认成了寿司外卖员。而有些人赞扬我的法语“口音十分纯正”；甚至有人为了取悦我，而说我是“可爱的中国人”。（翻译自Frédéric Chau，2015：22。Frédéric Chau是有中国和柬埔寨血统、出生在越南的法国演员。）

自从18世纪民族国家和护照诞生以来，国籍就一直盛行至今，“本土”和“非本土”的二分法也是一样。在大部分关于海外留学的研究中，学者发现，学生在海外学习期间，比如在海外做交换生或攻读学位时，大部分人不愿意与来自同一国家的人交流，而是更喜欢和当地人交流或者交朋友。很多人害怕别人发现他们与来自同一国家的人“粘在一起”。我们创造了这样一种世界观，即跨越国界意味着选择那些不同的人，尤其是来自本土的人，一个“真正的当地人”。而“本土”这个词的问题常常与其判断标准有关：我们是根据出生地点、国籍或语言来定义一个地方，还是根据这个人住在某个地方这个简单事实来定义？我们的社会中有很多迹象表明，我们痴迷于这种“本土”，“正宗的”本土。

几年前，我一个朋友来到芬兰，想让我为她组织一些“典型的”芬兰活动。因为我自己并不太相信是否有这种活动，于是我去了旅游中心进行咨询。他们给了我一本小册子，里面包含着不同的旅游活动。其中一页上推荐了两项活动。第一个是去赫尔辛基动物园看有“异国情调”的动物。第二个则是到某些人的家里去：

> 你是否在芬兰人自己的家里见过他们？这是一个难得的机会，我们能帮助你真正了解芬兰人和当地的生活方式。
>
> 芬兰人喜欢喝咖啡配点心。现在你也可以坐在咖啡桌旁，和克鲁努哈卡人好好聊聊，克鲁努哈卡是市中心最古老的地方之一。在访问当地家庭时，你也能有机会聊一聊当前时事和芬兰文化。

对这场活动（必须付费）的描述十分符合笔者现在所讨论的问题。为什么游客要花钱去参观别人的家，边喝咖啡边讨论时事和文化呢？是因为游客很难见到当地人，还是因为人们希望他们能见到当地人？对这场活动的描述似乎更证实了它能带来原汁原味、独一无二的享受。它被描述为一个“难得的机会”，“能有机会去”。它将当地生活说成是“单一的”（“本地的生活方式”“芬兰文化”），证明了我们之前所提到的跨文化性带有局限性的本质主义形式。最后，最为重要的一点是，旅游的地点是（1）赫尔辛基的市中心，而不是在郊区，（2）是芬兰首都赫尔辛基最富裕的地区之一。这就是为什么向游客“表演”芬兰风情的人既不能代表“芬兰人”，也不能代表“当地的生活方式”。将这种想象的“单一性”兜售给游客是很危险的，因为这只向游客展现了芬兰多元人口的一面：芬兰还有男人/女人/其他人，年轻人/老年人，穷人/富人/其他人，等等。

同样在几年前，芬兰红十字会为想要学习如何与“移民”交朋友的人组织了一门课程，主要是为了训练那些可以见到和帮助芬兰“难民”的人。我把移民和难民打上引号，是因为组织者常常会混用这两个词。我申请了这门课程，但被拒绝了，因为我不是纯正的芬兰人。他们说我无法帮助他们了解芬兰文化，也无法帮助他们“融入”芬兰社会。我对此提出了抗议，因为我在这个国家已经生活了20多年，我觉得自己和其他芬兰人一样有能力成为“难民”的“朋友”，帮助他们脱离困境。我的联系人通过电子邮件告诉我，他们不希望难民因为有一个非“纯正的”的芬兰朋友而感到失望，他们更希望与当地人交朋友。我对这句话感到生气和沮丧，但是最后，他们还是很不情愿地录取了我。

最后，让我再分享一个关于“本土”的例子。我的一个朋友把她的孩子送到德国三个星期，让他们学习德语和“文化”。孩子们将住在寄宿家庭里。第一天晚上，当母亲和孩子们交谈时，她意识到寄宿家庭并不像她想象的那样，因为这一家的家长来自土耳其。于是我的朋友立即联系了安排这次住宿的中介（她花了一大笔钱），请他找一个“真正的”当地德国家庭，而不是（我引用）“移民家庭”。中介同意了，为她找到了一个“典型的”德国白人家庭。

看完这些例子后，我们有必要反思一下这个问题：谁有权利说谁可以作为一个“本地人”或“非本地人”？可以根据语言、宗教和起源来决定吗？为什么不能让人们自己决定呢？如果一个人出生在国外，难道他就不能有一天成为当地人吗？可以将“本地人”和“非本地人”之间的等级划分合理合法化吗？这种划分是长久不变的吗？

芬兰每年都会选出“最佳新芬兰人”，主要对象是获得芬兰国籍的移民。我常常好奇，如果他们被选为年度“最佳新芬兰人”的话，那么“新”这个标签会在他们身上贴多久呢。

问题

1. 你能举出历史中全球化的例子吗？

2. 人们通常对你的国家有什么样的想象？你对其他国家有什么想象？

3. 想想你认识的另一个国家的人：说出五个你和她/他的共同点。

4. 你知道关于你的国家国民起源的不同理论吗？

5. 本章中，我认为每个人都是多样化的。你如何理解这一点？你自己在哪些方面是多样化的？

参考文献

ABDALLAH-PRETCEILLE M. Vers une pédagogie interculturelle [M]. Paris：Economica，1986.

AMSELLE J. L. Branchements：Anthropologie de l’universalité des cultures [M]. Paris：Champs Flammarion，2001.

ANDERSON B. Imagined communities：Refl ections on the origin and spread of nationalism [M]. London: Verso, 1983.

APPADURAI A. Fear of small numbers: An essay on the geography of anger [M]. Durham: Duke University Press, 2006.

ARENDT H. The human condition [M]. Chicago: The University of Chicago Press, 1958.

BAUMAN Z. The making and unmaking of strangers [M]// P. Werbner &T. Modood (Eds.) . Debating cultural hybridity. London: Zed Books, 1997.

BAUMAN Z. Identity [M]. Cambridge: Polity Press, 2004.

BHATIA S. Interpreting the meanings of schooling, hybridity, and multicultural citizenship in diaspora communities [J]. Yearbook of the National Society for the Study of Education, 2010, 109 (1) : 66–81.

CASTORIADIS C. The imaginary institution of society [M]. Cambridge: Polity Press, 1987.

CHAU F. Je viens de si loin [M]. Paris: Philippe Rey, 2015.

COMAROFF J. L. & COMAROFF J. Ethnicity, inc. [M]. Chicago: The University of Chicago Press, 2009.

DE SINGLY F. Libres ensemble [M]. Paris: Livre de Poche, 2003.

DE SOUSA SANTOS B. Graduation address McGill University [J]. Référence, 2012, 58 (1) : 230–241.

DERVIN F. A plea for change in research on intercultural discourses: A 'liquid' approach to the study of the acculturation of Chinese students [J]. Journal of Multicultural Discourses, 2011, 6 (1) : 37–52.

DERVIN F. Towards post-intercultural teacher education: Analysing 'extreme' Intercultural dialogue to reconstruct interculturality [J]. European

Journal of Teacher Education, 2015, 38(1): 71–86.

DURKHEIM E. The elementary forms of religious life [M]. New York: Free Press, 1995.

FOUCAULT M. Technologies of the self [M]. London: Tavistock, 1982.

GONZÁLEZ-VÉLEZ M. Assessing the conceptual use of social imagination in media research [J]. Journal of Communication Inquiry, 2002, 26(4): 349–353.

HAMID M. Discontent and its civilizations: Dispatches from Lahore, New York, and London [M]. New York: Riverhead Books, 2015.

HARRIS P. R., MORAN R. T. & MORAN S. V. Managing cultural differences [M]. Oxford: Butterworth-Heinemann, 2011.

HEINICH N. Le bêtisier du Sociologue [M]. Paris: Klinksieck, 2009.

HOLLIDAY A. Intercultural communication and ideology [M]. London: Sage, 2010.

HUNTINGTON S. P. The clash of civilizations and the remaking of world order [M]. New York: Simon & Schuster, 1996.

JULLIEN F. L'écart et l'entre: Leçon inaugurale de la Chaire sur l'altérité, 8 décembre 2011 [M]. Paris: Galilée, 2012.

KUREISHI H. The word and the bomb [M]. London: Faber and Faber, 2005.

KUREISHI H. Collected essays [M]. London: Faber and Faber, 2011.

LACAN J. Book XI: The four fundamental concepts of psychoanalysis [M]. New York: W.W. Norton and Company, 1977.

MAFFESOLI M. La contemplation du monde [M]. Paris: le Livre de

Poche, 1993.

MCDOWELL L. Spatializing feminism [M]// N. Duncan (Ed.) . BodySpace: Destabilising geographies of gender and sexuality. London: Routledge, 1996.

MOGHADDAM F. M. Multiculturalism and intergroup relations: Implications for democracy in a global context [M]. Washington, DC: American Psychological Association Press, 2008.

NIEMI P. M., KUUSISTO A. & KALLIONIEMI A. Discussing school celebrations from an intercultural perspective — A study in the Finnish context [J]. Intercultural Education, 2014, 25 (4) : 255–268.

PIETERSE J. N. Globalization and culture: Global mélange [M]. Lanham: Rowman and Littlefi eld Publishers, 2004.

RIVZI F. Beyond the social imaginary of 'clash of civilizations'? [J]. Educational Philosophy and Theory, 2011, 43 (3) : 225–235.

SAID E. Representations of the intellectual [M]. New York: Vintage Books, 1993.

SAID E. The clash of ignorance [J/OL]. The Nation, 2001: 1–5 [2001-10-22]. http: //www.thenation. com/article/clash-ignorance/.

SAID E. From Oslo to Iraq and the road map [J]. NOEL B. SALAZAR. Tourism imaginaries: A conceptual approach. Annals of Tourism Research, 2012, 39 (2) : 863–882.

SEN A. The argumentative Indian [M]. London: Penguin, 2005.

SIMMEL G. Journal posthume [M]. Paris: Circé, 2013.

SPECTOR T. Identically different [M]. New York: Phoenix, 2012.

SUBRAHMANYAM S. Three ways to be alien: Travails and encounters in the early modern world (The Menahem Stern Jerusalem Lectures) [M]. Waltham: Brandeis University Press, 2011.

TAYLOR C. Modern social imaginaries [M]. Durham: Duke University Press, 2004.

WIKAN U. Generous betrayal [M]. Chicago: Chicago University Press, 2002.

WONG P. P. The life of a banana [M]. London: Legend Times Group, 2014.

WOOD P. Diversity: The invention of a concept [M]. San Francisco: Encounter Books, 2003.

第四章　他者化论断

摘　要："他者化"（Othering）是教育领域跨文化交际中常见的现象，指人们在遇到或谈论别人时，对别人的刻板印象和表面印象。本章讨论了关于他者化的定义，并说明了他者化这一现象是不稳定的。笔者运用了语言学工具来帮助我们分析他者化的相关论断，试图深入理解背后隐含的民族中心主义、（隐藏的）种族主义和（隐藏的）仇外心理。旨在让通过某种工具考察跨文化、身份与政治的教育者和研究人员，也会对本章内容感兴趣。

> 一个人在学校学到的东西并不总是学校认为它在教授的东西。（Rushdie，2012：31）

几年前，欧洲一所著名大学中的一名黑人"本地"学生惊讶地发现，他的照片被用在学校的网站上以宣传这所大学的"国际化"。对此他说道：

> 这太奇怪了：如果学校要宣传其研究实力，就该展示穿白大褂

的人。如果学校要宣传它的图书馆，就该展示好多书。如果学校要宣传它的国际化，不知道为什么展示了我。

2015年，我自己的大学发起了一场我认为同样具有争议性的广告运动，其目标在于将它的“品牌”推广到全世界。运动中包括了许多“不同寻常”之人的图片：一位头上戴着卷心菜的年轻白人，一位白人老妇人背着一个白人婴儿，一位红头发的白人妇女，头上戴着一个看起来像恐龙蛋似的东西，还有一个丑陋的白人科学家——他们看起来快乐而自信。图片上还有另外两个“多样性”的人物：一位头戴向日葵的黑人妇女，面带微笑，还有一个亚洲模样的孩子，看起来很悲伤，头上顶着一块正在融化的冰。我对最后一幅图片的内容感到十分困惑：其他的画都是那么积极——充满了“白人”，为什么唯一那幅关于亚洲孩子的画，却在他的头上有一个象征腐朽星球的符号呢？难道这里要传达的他者化的信息是：只有亚洲要对很可能即将到来的灾难负责，而“西方”（以我的大学为代表）将帮助他们解决这个棘手的问题？但事实上“西方”是否也要为这个问题负责呢？

谁是他者？

他者一直是历史中的重要角色，由不同的标签定义：古希腊的野蛮人（Barbarian：一种喃喃细语的拟声词）、十七世纪的（高贵的）野蛮人，二十一世纪的（激进的）另类。16世纪西班牙殖民和征服美洲期间，巴利亚多利德辩论对新大陆美洲印第安人的地位问题进行了讨论，形成了两大对立阵营：这些他者应该被当作人还是奴隶来对待？直到今天，这些问题还反复出现在世界各地（澳大利亚的移民、美国和欧洲的人种动物园、南非的种族隔离制度以及达尔富尔战争等等）。虽然他者形象不是一模一样的，但事实上，人们在对待或谈及各种各样的他者的方式上是存在等级划分的。例如在欧洲，某些移民比其他移民受到更好的待遇，取决于他们的来源、经济资本和语言。对于Tseëlon（2001：5）来说：

> 现代性痴迷于秩序和命令，以民族国家为代表，创造了一个文化同质的神话。…… 因此，民族国家成为了身份的源头，让人既纠结又排斥。通过在自我周围设置界限，人们也定义了非自我（局内人/局外人，熟人/陌生人）。

他者也是我们之中的一员。许多名人都曾书写过对他者的理解。希腊哲学家亚里士多德说过："过于自信的人需要通过友谊来了解自己"（《大伦理学》）；法国诗人亚瑟·兰波有句名言："我是另一个人"（1871，2002：35）；最近，苏格兰精神病学家R.D. Laing强调："每个人对别人来说都是他者"（1967）。

他者及其衍生概念他者性都是典型的跨学科概念。比如说，人们在心理学、社会学、哲学、人类学、语言学以及神学、考古学、历史学和性别研究等不同领域都对这一概念有所涉及。事实上，自18世纪以来，"他者"一直是人文社会科学的核心概念。例如，从人类学学科的建立到第二次世界大战结束，"异域的"他者一直是这一学科研究的重点。今天，在对过去多年人类学工作的讨论和批判后，大多数人类学家开始研究全球化的社会，尽量不再把他们的观察对象殊异化。"他者"在哲学，特别是本体论（存在论）范畴，也是一个研究重点。自后结构主义/后现代主义的出现，以及20世纪80年代以来标志着全球化时代的归属危机出现以来，人们对他者和他者性的研究兴趣似乎呈指数增长。除了“异域的他者”之外，不同的“他者”形象也引起了全世界媒体和文学作品的关注（例如，性少数群体、残疾人等等）。

“他者化”的概念源于社会中他人的存在。实际上，它也与身份的概念有很大关系（见第二章）。他者化是指将泛泛的其他人转化为某个他者，从而在不同与相同、局内人与局外人之间形成界限。在语言的交流和情感的互动中，形成了导致“他者化”的情感和认知机制。在Chebel d’appollonia（2011：11）看来，“他者化”相当于“身份的标本剥制者”，因为“他者化”会限制人们对于“她是谁”和“她代表什么”的理解。

在心理学中，他者化是每个人都经历的普通过程：为了生存，一个人需要理解他人，因此一个人他者化别人，就像别人他者化我们自己一样。他者化只能通过在语篇中断裂或连接自我与他者来实现。为了分清他者，人们需要将自己与他人进行比较，或者将自己所在的群体与另一个群体进行比较，反之亦然。

在社会学中，他者化指的是能够在“我们”和“他们”之间区分出道德高低和政治优劣的界限。在这种对他者化的理解中，权力总是被用来代表他者和自我。他者总是被描述为“有缺陷的”，认为她不如“我们”优秀或能干，这就会导致刻板印象和其他形式的表面印象。我们常常会在媒体、公众话语，甚至在学术研究中（Krumer-Nevo和Sidi，2012）发现这种情况。文学理论家Edward Said（1978）在他关于东方主义（Orientalism）的研究中，运用了一种宏观的方法来研究“他者”，他在书中论证了东方世界的表面印象（尤其是中东）是如何被认为是被动的、神秘的、低等的，这使得西方主义者能够用正面的语词来定义自己。

他者化会涉及到各种各样的身份标记：国籍、种族、语言、宗教、性别等等。他者化往往伴随着这样一种观点，即一些群体常常被非人化或妖魔化，因为他们被认为是低人一等的。然而在一个“无权无势”的群体内部，他者化也会通过自我他者化发生。例如说，非裔美国人和亚裔美国人会分别使用“奥利奥”（黑色饼干和白色夹心的三明治饼干）和“香蕉”，指代皮肤是黑色/黄色，但骨子里却是个典型白人的人。在某些情况下，自我他者化可以作为一种保护自我、获取权威，甚至要求特殊权利的方式——这并不总是一件好事，尤其在他人权利受到侵犯的情况下。某些宗教、文化和性少数群体（彩虹族群）的发言人并不总是代表“多数”，他们有自己的想法。他们构建的身份形象并不总是与他们的同胞一致，而这些同胞就会觉得自己被这些发言人“他者化”了。

随着现代性在18世纪欧洲的诞生，国家身份成为了“他者化”最为有力的工具，这导致了去殖民化/新殖民、世界大战和纳粹大屠杀的发生。在今天，尽管民族国家失去了一些权力，通过制造身份来获得经济价值，比如国家品牌化或把国家当作企业一样进行旅游推广，仍会导致某些形式的“他者化”，这种“他者”是人为制造的，经常反复利用老掉牙的刻板印象，或再创造出新的印象。

在教育领域中，他者化已经成为一种需要被公开讨论、摒弃或抗争的现象，因为它会导致种族主义、性别歧视甚至是偏执。与此同时，Britain A. Hart的一篇反对教育种族主义的报告告诉我们，教育工作者本身是如何通过推进一项带有缺陷的反种族主义行动，来制造他者化论断的：

> 我拍了一段视频，视频中我的同事们担任儿童戏剧导师，他们（自认为）正在帮助孩子们接受自己的种族身份并对此感到自豪。当

孩子们被问到“我们有时把自己定义为白人、黑人、亚洲人或混血儿——你怎么定义你自己?”时，一个男孩回答得含含糊糊（但很大声地说）。“啊，一个黑皮肤的人吧”，戏剧导师说道。“不，是一个跳舞的人”，男孩说。

给人贴标签这件事，就算是带着最大的尊重和忍耐，也会轻易导致他者化，或像上面这段摘录一样，错误地将他人“定性”。对许多研究者来说，“国民教育”常会用来制造他者化，决定谁符合谁不符合。而且这种情况并不像人们所想的那样，仅仅发生在“西方”。来自尼日利亚的Lammin-Sullay Sesay（1996：22—23）在他的小说中讲述了他作为一名芬兰国际学生的经历：

我还记得地理课上我们用过的一本书，是Charles McIntyre的《世界地域和人口》。正是通过这本书，我第一次了解了斯堪的纳维亚半岛和芬兰。那时我可能是12或14岁。这段时间里，当我们学习到上述地区时，很少会提到这些地方是高度工业化和高度发展的事实。其实事实上，除了一点环境保护或测量天气的先进技术以外，我从未意识到，这里的人受教育程度很高，住的房子很好。如果这个地方真的那么冷，冬天那么糟糕，我们很快会想到这里的生活一定非常原始。这是真的，因为我们的地理老师多多少少总是把重点放在解释这里的气候条件。他们不会浪费时间说这里是否有电力设备或雪上摩托车，或是飞机是否敢飞来这里。来到芬兰以后，我发现我在芬兰接受的这种不带感情的关于“冻土地带”的教育，和芬兰孩子接受关于非洲的教育时，几乎是一模一样。说到非洲，老师就只会谈到饥荒的危害、原始的乡村以及四处弥漫的苦难和贫乏。长久以来，我一直觉得非常费解，为什么每个社会中的学校老师总是倾向和习惯于向孩子们讲授每个社会的严酷特征，却忽视或隐匿了每个社会存在着的真实的优点呢?

最后，我曾在香港目睹了一场非常有趣的“冲突”，一个看起来像印度人的人在一家餐馆抱怨服务员的服务，声称服务员“粗鲁”而“傲慢”。他把这位服务员与中国大陆的服务员进行比较后，非常生气，因为他没想到香港人会比大陆人还“粗鲁”…… 排他化绝对是一种普遍的罪恶 ……

他者化是一种不稳定的现象

他者化是一种复杂的现象，可能随着时间的推移而改变，这取决于特定背景下集体意识形态和主体间共同建构的意识形态如何演变。非洲奴隶的例子说明：16世纪的美洲，他们先是被视为异教徒，而1680年之后，他们又被贴上“黑鬼”的标签（Wimmer，2013：8）。有些人一直被困在他们的他者性之中（如欧洲的吉普赛人），而其他的“他者们”则能在被定义为他者的几十年后享受更多积极的东西（如二战后在芬兰避难的卡累利阿人）。

生于罗马尼亚的法国社会心理学家Moscovici（1961）提出的（社会）表征概念有助于我们理解他者化。表征是一系列人类共享的价值、思想和实践体系，使人们能够理解自己的世界并与他人互动（Moscovici，1961）。这正是“他者化”社会交往中所允许的。上面描述的现象是通过自我、他者和环境之间的表征（共同）建构和（重新）协商而发生的。在全球化的世界里，由于意义越来越难以确定，他者化也变得越来越难以预测，因此表征也变得越来越复杂。这所带来的影响包括：比如我们遇到一个看起来像亚洲人的人，但实际上他与我们出生在同一个国家，我们的母语是相同的。

他者化也会用于其他的方面。人们用它来定位自己，保护自己，取悦/引诱他人，决定（共同的/不同的）身份，保护自己免受歧视或被边缘化，或对他人产生更好的感觉。他者化也会使人们通过想象他人来（重新）创造和理解自我。在充满不确定性的后现代时代，很容易看出他者化和政治身份是多么的不稳定。

文学作品中也包含了各种形式的他者化。就“民族的”和“文化的”他者而言，人们常常会使用下列标签：本质主义、种族主义、新种族主义（将文化作为种族的傀儡；Dhamoon，2009）、文化主义（将文化作为对一切的解释）、民族中心主义、异国情调、伊斯兰恐惧症、东方主义（Orientalism）、西方主义（Occidentalism）。尤其是在未来，当世界力量发生转移时，非西方人士如何看待西方和反东方主义，或者东方人如何使用东方学的期望来他者化自己（Dervin和Gao，2012），是需要重点研究的他者化的两种不同形式，随着民族国家影响力的丧失，东西方的二分法再次出现，成为了区分西方人和东方人的一种方式。像所有的标签一样，这两个词需要去结构化。在教育方面，东方常常与某些消极的特征（死记硬背、缺乏批判性等）联系在一起，而西方则保有更多积极的特征。以中国学生出国留学为例，我们经常会看到这种描述：“集体主义社会”（如中国）的学生会学习“如何做”，而个人主义社会（如英国）的学生会学习“如何学习”，或是很多来自集体主义文化的人，很难接受放下自己文化身份的观念。Sen（2005：129）严厉谴责了这种高人一等、带有民族中心主义色彩的言论，他写道："鉴于世界历史上文化和智力的相互联系，我们很难判断什么是'西方的'而什么不是。"Holliday（2010）也非常批判对个人主义和集体主义的论断。在这位学者看来，"尽管声称是保持中立的，但很明显能看出，个人主义代表想象中的正面特征，而集体主义代表想象中的负面特征"（Holliday，2010：9）。

所有这些他者化的跨文化形式，毫无中立可言，且都有以下缺点：他们只关注人与人之间的差异，而忽略了这样一个事实：即使来自不同的地方，说着不同的语言，人们仍有很多相似之处；他们人为地划定人与人之间的界限；对文化、宗教和种族的描述往往是片面和笼统的；他们让人觉得，只有一个人的文化、种族或宗教才会影响他的观点、行为和态度。他者化的某些论述还导致了诸如仇恨、杀戮、恐怖主义、奴役、种族灭绝等可怕的行为。在日常交往中，他者化也易导致偏见、权力失衡/歧视（我的文化/宗教比你的好），以及傲慢的态度（他者是有缺陷的）。

他者化话语分析

鉴于他者化是一个跨学科话题，因此分析他者化话语的方法是多角度多方面的。这里提出了两种社会建构主义的视角，以资镜鉴。

第一个方法取自R. Dhamoon 2009年出版的《身份/差异政治》一书。Dhamoon是一位研究哲学和政治学的学者。通过研究加拿大是如何论述多元文化主义的，她建议研究应该从对意义制造政治的批判下手，以及权力（而不是文化）是如何导致差异和他者化的论断，又将产生哪些影响等。通过这样做，她把他者化置于研究的中心（地位）。Dhamoon在她的分析中，提出了多个问题：在不同的社会背景下，如何通过话语来构建不同的社会界线？话语如何与权力关系相联系？谁和什么被描述为（非）正常和优劣的？（2009：11）。Dhamoon的方法与其他领域两位学者所使用的方法非常相似。社会语言学家Ingrid Piller也提出了研究跨文化交际中他者化问题的社会建构主义方法。她建议人们在分析数据时应提出以下问题（2011：17）："谁在说话？说话者或写作者是可识别的个人或机构吗？他们以什么角色说话或写作？目标受众是谁？有人偷听吗？如果有互动的话，他们各自的反应是什么？相关的背景是什么？例如说，互动对象之间的关系是内容、时间和地点还是媒介？提及文化的目的是什么？"此外，Breidenbach和Nyíri（2009）在《文化无处不在》专栏中，当质疑"文化声明和权利动机背后或明或暗的假设可能被隐藏"时，也提出了类似的方法（2009：340）。以下是他们的建议，即我们应该扪心自问的问题（2009：343）："文化背后关于某个群体或明或暗的论断是什么？在哪个点上，这些群体被定义和区分出去呢？……谁在制造关于文化的论断？他们为什么要这么做呢？"

这些学者的共同之处在于，都热衷于通过考察权力差异的影响，在关于文化或对他人态度的言辞中解构他者化的话语。然而，Dhamoon（2009）似乎是唯一一个在研究中重视交叉性这个重要特征的人。她将其定义为"经济、政治、文化、心理、主观和经验等多种差异在特定历史语境中交叉时所产生的复杂的、不可简化的、多样的和可变的影响"（2009：61）。她所传达的信息颇为重要：为了检验多元文化主义、他者和他者化的行为，我们必须考虑不止一个身份标记。比如，除了只将文化当作推动他者化的唯一因素外，我们更应考虑到种族、性别、阶级、族群、残疾、性向等一系列因素在人们识别和区分他人时的作用（2009：63）。Dhamoon恰恰也是这样做的，在其"种族化的性别划分"一章中，她以加拿大穆斯林妇女为研究对象，观察性别化的种族分化是如何构建关于东方主义、伊斯兰恐惧症、欧洲中心主义性别歧视等“混合的”的话语的（2009：132）。为了加深我们对他者化的全面理解和分析，交叉性应该是重要的一个步骤。

如前所述，识别这些不同的声音对研究者来说是一个挑战，特别是当他们想要“更深入地”挖掘数据，从对他者化过程的描述更进一步，同时说明这些话语的不稳定性时，更加艰难。在这种情况下，以巴赫金的对话主义（Dialogism）（1982）为代表，以及受巴赫金、米德和黑格尔的启发所发起的跨学科研究运动，特别是关于“对话塑造自我”（Dialogical Self）的研究方法，就显得非常有用。对话主义主要基于他者性是一切的中心这一论断（巴赫金，1982）。换句话说，在分析诸如知识、社会和主观性等动态的、情境化的现象时，对话应该是分析的基本单位（Gillespie and Cornish，2010：15）。此外，分析中应充分考虑到所考察的现象发生时的社会、历史和文化背景。巴赫金的理论将声音的概念置于话语的中心。Roulet（2011：209）将这位俄罗斯哲学家的思想总结如下：

> —— 话语和社会的多种声音之间存在持续的相互作用；
>
> —— 话语总是与以前的话语和声音联系在一起的；
>
> —— 话语都是对先前话语的反应，因此与这些话语共同组成对话；
>
> —— 其他人因此总是出现在人们说的话中。

因此，分析他者化的话语需要考察上述因素。在Grossen（2010：7）看来，“对话法的关键要素之一就是，语言在本质上是多义的，它的意义不是由语言代码提前确定好的，而是在特定的语境中构建起来的”。这意味着在研究方法方面，我们应该使用能够突出主体间性的方法（Gillespie和Cornish，2010）。从语言学上讲，对话主义是以特定语言标记或形式的出现为标志的（代词，比如“我们”；转述的话语；被动语态；等等）。对话主义者将转述的话语（直接或间接的）称为话语表征（Roulet，2011：210），因为从另一个语境中被转述，它就代表了话语和行动。反讽、否定等特定现象，以及诸如“但是”等特定话语标记的使用，都标志着对话主义。这些例子取自Roulet（2011：215—216）：

——（在明显失败的情况下说的）：真了不起！（讽刺）

—— 保罗是个大块头；但他一点也不强壮（否定）。

在M. Grossen（在）2010年发表的文章中，她反问自己，研究者是否能够、以及如何能够开发出适合分析对话的工具，尤其是在并非所有的有用声音都能够被识别的情况下。尽管她的结论证实，复杂的理论和工具之间存在差距且不易填满，但她的文章为我们回答Dhamoon、Piller、Breidenbach和Nyíri提出的如何检验他者化的问题提供了一些线索。她的第一个提议是使用语言学方法来展示话语是如何从一个话语者转移到另一个话语者，以及话语是如何被整合和再创造的（2010：17）：例如，人称代词的转换，话语者的地位（教师、女性、医生……）和争论不休的矛盾。法国语用学很好地补充了对话主义方法。Johansson和Suomela-Salmi（2011：71）解释说：“语用学是从不同语言要素的角度来处理说话层面的意义。换句话说，话语者的行为是重点：一方面，说话的人会在话语中留下痕迹和标识；另一方面，话语者和对话者之间也存在一定关系。”简而言之，语用学方法的旨趣在于（1）一个人如何建构她/他的话语，和（2）他/她如何与他人协商这段话语（主体间性）。语用学的核心是要将话语者视为一个异质的主体，将自己置于他人的位置上，从而使用和管理各种话语策略和实用策略来构建自我、他人、环境、经验等等。这常常是以一种无计划、无系统、多变化的方式进行的。

最著名的法国语用学代表人物包括Émile Benveniste，Antoine Culioli，Oswald Ducrot和Catherine Kerbrat- Orechionni（Johansson 和 Suomela-Salmi，2011）。他们认为许多不同的语言要素被用来分析话语。指示词（人、时间和空间的标记词，如人称代词、副词和动词）等语言要素能够帮助话语者“在话语中展示自我或清楚地表达自我，或是在话语中疏远自己，不留下存在的一丝痕迹或明确表明自己的态度”（Johansson和Suomela-Salmi，2011：94）。这同样适用于话语情态，它可以给我们提供线索，了解话语者对他/她所说的话的态度（副词、转折词等等）。例如，道义情态标示着责任，与道德和社会规范相关（例如，你必须这样做；Johansson 和 Suomela-Salmi，2011：97）。名词也可以表达话语者对人、现象、物体等的态度（保罗是个懒汉）。因此我们很容易看出，语用标记可以帮助研究者分析人们如何在交流中一方面共同构建他们是谁，一方面揭示他们对这些场景的情感。通过研究话语中的语用变化，语用学还可以帮助我们区分不稳定因素：转折、矛盾、修正、潜在操控等。

最后一个问题是在人们的话语和构建的东西中辨识多种声音的可能性：他者的声音，他们自己过去/未来的声音等。Gillespie和Cornish（2010）也从对话的角度进行研究，建议将主体间性作为分析的重点。因此，他们建议要摒弃个人主义的研究方法，即忽视他者化的话语是人与人共同建构的这一事实（2010：3）。这将有助于考察在他者化交流过程的不稳定性以及其形成的复杂性。

问题

1. 你同意他者化是“普遍的罪恶”这一观点吗？你认为一个人不能没有它吗？

2. 上次别人公然将你他者化是什么时候？他们是如何做到的，为什么这样做？同样，你上一次将别人他者化是什么时候？

3. 很明显，有些人更容易被他者化。在你周围，这些都是什么人呢？

4. 你能想到在媒体中无处不在的某些团体/少数族群的某个发言人吗？问问这些团体里的其他人，他们对发言人和他/她代表的内容有什么想法？

5. 你如何定义文化主义的概念？

参考文献

BAKHTIN M. M. The dialogic imagination [M]. Austin: University of Texas Press, 1982.

BREIDENBACH J. & NYÍRI P. Seeing culture everywhere [M]. Washington: University of Washington Press, 2009.

CHEBEL D'APPOLLONIA A. Les frontières du racisme [M]. Paris: Presses de Sciences Po, 2011.

DERVIN F. A plea for change in research on intercultural discourses: A 'liquid' approach to the study of the acculturation of Chinese students [J]. Journal of Multicultural Discourses, 2011, 6(1): 37–52.

DERVIN F. & GAO, M. Keeping up appearances before the 'other'?

Interculturality and occidentalism in the educational TV-programme Happy Chinese [J]. Frontiers of Education in China, 2012, 7(4), 553–575.

DHAMOON R. Identity/difference politics: How difference is produced and why it matters [M]. Vancouver: UBC Press, 2009.

GILLESPIE A. & CORNISH F. Intersubjectivity: Towards a dialogical analysis [J]. Journal for the Theory of Social Behaviour, 2010, 40: 19–46.

GROSSEN M. Interaction analysis and psychology: A dialogical perspective [J]. Integrative Psychological and Behavioural Sciences, 2010, 44 (1): 1–22.

HART A. The anti-racist policy and the regulation of school life [M]. London: Manifesto Club, 2013.

HOLLIDAY A. Intercultural communication and ideology [M]. London: Sage, 2010.

JOHANSSON M. & SUOMELA-SALMI E. Enonciation: French pragmatic approach (es) [M]// Jan Zienkowski. Discursive pragmatics. Amsterdam: Benjamins, 2010.

KRUMER-NEVO M. & SIDI M. Writing against othering [J]. Qualitative Inquiry, 2012, 18: 299–309.

LAING R.D. The politics of experience and the bird paradise [M]. Harmondsworth: Penguin, 1967.

MOSCOVICI S. La psychanalyse, son image et son public [M]. Paris: P.U.F, 1961.

PILLER I. Intercultural communication: A critical introduction [M]. Edinburgh: EUP, 2011.

RIMBAUD A. The drunken boat [M]. New York: Two Rivers Press, 1871.

ROULET E. Polyphony [M]//Jan Zienkowski. Discursive pragmatics. Amsterdam: Benjamins, 2011.

RUSHDIE S. Joseph Anton: A memoir [M]. New York: Random House, 2012.

SAID E. Orientalism [M]. London: Penguin, 1978.

SEN A. The argumentative Indian [M]. London: Penguin, 2005.

Sesay L. S. Messages from Finland [M]. Turku: Reindeer Books, 1996.

TSEËLON E. (Ed.). Masquerade and identities: Essays on gender, sexuality and marginality [M]. London: Routledge, 2001.

WIMMER A. Ethnic boundary making: Institutions, power, networks [M]. Oxford: Oxford University Press, 2013.

第五章　跨文化性与人权的“脆弱”

摘　要：许多对跨文化性的讨论是基于人权角度的。本章建议跳出人权主义，跳出这种以欧洲为中心来探讨人权的天真方式。某些超国家的行动因其“脆弱性”，以及将“我们”和“他们”置于人权之中，而受到了批判。教育领域将对与上述方法“背道而驰”的反霸权方式的讨论，作为本章的结论。

我生活和工作在一个常常名列国际前茅的国家：全球媒体自由指数（2009年）第1名，《新闻周刊》“世界最佳国家”（2010年）第1名，“世界好国家”（2014年）第2名，“最适合妈妈居住的国家”（2010年）第7名，全球和平指数（2010年）第7名。此外，芬兰还在“2015年世界自由指数”（自由评级、公民自由、政治权利）中获得最高分。因此，北欧国家常常被人们视为“乌托邦”，尤其是在平等、社会公平、民主以及人权方面。然而这个神话还有着另外一面。根据国际特赦组织2013年的一份报告，芬兰许多方面侵犯了人权（或助长了许多侵犯人权的行为）。2011年，这个拥有500万居民的小国向25个不尊重欧盟人权标准的国家出口了武器。例如，芬兰国防部门同意向哈萨克斯坦这个媒体自由和人权经常受到侵犯的国家出口步枪和弹药。其他例子包括：（1）难民没有被安置在适当的地方而是被收留在警察局，并和面临刑事指控的犯罪嫌疑人待在一起。（2）对妇女和女童的暴力行为是个严重问题。（3）警察拘留期间过度使用武力的相关报道很多。（4）良知反战者拒服兵役遭到监禁，其未来会遭受歧视和影响（比如未来不能当公务员）。然而新闻媒体、芬兰人民或是每年到访的成百上千名“示范游客”很少会注意和批评芬兰的人权问题，因为他们根本不知道有这些问题的存在，而且已经被这个国家的“美好”洗脑了。（Dervin，2013）。

芬兰经常向其他国家提供有关平等、民主和人权的课程。这很容易导致种族中心主义（对他人隐性和/或显性的优越感）（LeVine and Campbell，1972）和沾沾自喜（我们在帮助他人并且不需要他人的帮助时；De Oliveira，2011）。跨文化在这里可以理解为来自不同国家的人的相处，但一定要记得，每个人不仅代表着一种“文化”，还代表着相互交错的不同社会阶层、性别、年代和宗教，这是一个需要高度关注的问题。本章对处理跨文化对话时人权话语的霸权性提出质疑（De Sousa Santos，2015），并提出要将上述要素纳入“反霸权方式”。Boaventura de Sousa Santos（2009：n.p.）认为：“在这个时代，对人权进行理论化并不容易。人权被认为是应对世界上各种问题的有效方案，几乎对任何事都有效。但现在，人们越来越发现，人权对于我们的时代并不那么有效，甚至可以说，这是一个问题尖锐、答案无力的人权时代。”关于芬兰的一些例子足以证明我的论点。

自1948年《世界人权宣言》获得联合国大会批准通过以来，有关人权的论述已在“国际法、全球性和区域性机构、各国（主要指自由民主制国家）的外交政策，以及各种各样不断增长的非政府组织和网络活动中”（Beitz，2011：1）盛行起来。简言之，人权有“道德生活”“法律生活”和“政治生活”（Beitz，2011：1）。为了避免历史中心主义或欧洲中心主义这样的“中心主义”，我们还需要牢记，人权是具有“历史生命”的（Beitz，2011：2）。例如，可以追溯到公元前六世纪的波斯塞勒斯圆筒（Cyrus Cylinder）通常被认为是历史上第一部人权宣言，它促进了不同民族和具有不同信仰的人之间的和谐（Mitchell，1988：83）。

《联合国宪章》（1945年）的创始成员国宣布：

> 教育应促进人格的全面发展、增强对人权和基本自由的尊重。它应促进所有国家、种族和宗教团体之间的理解、包容和友谊，并应推动联合国维护和平的活动。（第26条）

在教育领域，人权在过去几十年中扮演着重要角色，尤其与跨文化相关。因此，2008年欧盟关于跨文化对话的白皮书将跨文化教育同保障和发展人权、民主、法治以及增进相互理解并列为需要采取行动来维护和发展的五个关键领域之一，但是，教育中的“跨文化”在很大程度上仍被视为一种中立的信息交换与交流，而忽略了跨文化不仅包含且会助长不平衡的权力关系和差别待遇、滋生种族主义、文化主义、语言主义等各种主义的事实。这些代表了我认为是最“隐性”的侵犯人权的行为。继De Sousa Santos（2015：1）之后，我也认为跨文化教育很容易导致“世界上绝大多数居民（成为不了）人权的主体 …… 反而变成人权论述的客体”。本章会将上述方面进一步问题化。

超越单纯的人权主义？

许多学者指出，传统的人权概念（人权主义）因其被滥用而产生了问题。Mchangama和Verdirame（2014：n.p.）指出：如果人权是一种货币，那么过去几十年国际组织通过了海量的人权条约和无约束力的国际文书，造成了通货膨胀，导致人权的价值如自由落体般直线下降。经典的人权定义包含的方面太多，似乎总想涵盖“所有”，以至于这一概念难以管理。例如，Starkey（2003）认为，除经济、社会和文化权利外，人权还包括个人权利、人与人之间的关系权利，公共自由以及政治权利。正因为这种定义膨胀，以及定义的各方面缺乏交叉，在教育领域中有效开展人权工作成为一件难事。

与跨文化相关，De Sousa Santos（2015）对以下方面提出担忧：（1）人权“不管运用在任何社会、政治和文化背景下都普遍有效”的事实（2015：7）。（2）人权概念的建构通常基于“人类本质是个体性的、自我维持的，与非人类本质有质的不同”的观念（2015）。（3）哪些属于人权范畴由全球宣言、多边机构和北半球/西方世界的非政府组织来决定（2015）。（4）发展中国家的人权事务常被认为很成问题（北半球却很少；2015：49）。在社会学家看来，人权话语取决于权力并复制了权力的不对称性，这种不对称性源自“当代世界无序的新帝国主义、新殖民主义本质”（2009：n.p.）。他甚至认为，世界混乱的某些代表与其说是发展中国家人权话语中的主语，不如说是宾语；人类的许多苦难不能归罪于人权；许多侵犯人权的行为都是以人权的名义进行的（2015：78）。在提升尊严的同时，“西方”的人权概念也推动了帝国主义，扩散了不幸和苦难（2009：n.p.）。

1993年，联合国世界人权会议在奥地利举行，会上区分了西方和非西方对人权的解释（Friedman等，2005）。亚洲国家在1993年会议之前签署和发布的《曼谷宣言》对人权的普遍主义提出了批评：

> [各签署国]认识到，虽然人权在本质上具有普遍性，但它们必须放在不断变化的国际规则制定的演变进程中考量，同时还应关注到不同国家和地区的历史、文化和宗教背景的重要性。（Hamelink，1997：100）

让我举两个例子来说明，人权是如何或明或暗地被用来操纵关于自我和他人的话语，并由此划分了出于政治目的、不公正的等级制度。第一个例子，2014年，芬兰前总理在芬兰举办了“北方未来论坛”。他的特邀演讲嘉宾是时任英国首相戴维·卡梅伦：

> “英国、北欧国家和波罗的海国家的总理们将齐聚一堂交流意见，针对现代北欧经济面临的共同挑战寻找解决问题的新方法。北方未来论坛是独一无二的活动，汇集了9个北欧国家的总理、商界领袖、企业家和政策制定者。本论坛今年的讨论将集中在如何在当前的经济挑战下促进平等、幸福和竞争。会议还将介绍和讨论有助于与会国家创造就业和提高人民生活水平的政策、观点和创新。（http://nff2014.government.fi/about-northern-future-forum）

以下是卡梅伦在活动结束时发表的评论，很好地阐释了关于创新和竞争的新自由主义话语是如何被想象的“北欧”与中国和俄罗斯之间的比较所掩盖的。

> 最后对我来说，我认为我们是非常理性的北欧人，我们聚在一起讨论我们的问题以及面对的困难。我想我们也应该庆祝我们的成功，我认为值得庆祝的成功之一便是我深深相信我们的社会是开放、民主、自由、宽容、好辩、争鸣的社会，比起中国、俄罗斯等其他封闭的社会更有创新性和创造力。我认为我们应该庆祝，我们之所以能够保持领先地位，保持社会的创造性和认可度，保持人民源源不断的创造力，是因为我们经常谈论我们的问题，同时也肯定我们的价值，这些都是促进现在和未来繁荣发展的至关重要的部分。

有趣的是，卡梅伦想象了一个新的身份：北欧人。这个标签包括北欧国家、波罗的海国家和英国。这位英国首相将这个新类别定义为“非常理性”“开放”“民主”“自由”“宽容”“好辩”“争鸣”“有创新性”和“创造力”的，反对中国和俄罗斯这样“封闭”的社会，在西方和东方之间创造了一个新的等级制度。尽管“人权”一词并没有被提及为北欧人的“价值观”和“成就”之一，但上述许多特征暗示了它的存在：理性（“理性”的人尊重人权）、民主、宽容和开放（相对于封闭的社会）。尽管许多评论人士同意卡梅伦的观点，但我认为，这恰恰会导致沾沾自喜和自我满足，还会导致权力的不对称。正如引言中芬兰的例子所示，卡梅伦列出的许多与中国或俄罗斯相对的价值观，在芬兰这些地区也并不稳定。

第二个操纵对人权普遍性理解的例子，于2014年11月由芬兰媒体报导。虽然这个例子是处理同性婚姻，与“跨文化”的规范定义没有直接关系，但我发现这个例子与对人权的普遍性理解非常相关。彼时芬兰是最后几个没有批准同性婚姻的欧洲国家之一。时任内政部长和基督教民主联盟主席宣称她反对同性婚姻平等（*Yle News*，2014）。她的理由是基于1948年的《人权宣言》。她声称："联合国宣言是对人权普遍性理解的重要解读，宣言上说的是每个人都有权利……每个男人和女人都有结婚的权利，换句话说，宣言将婚姻定义为一个男人和一个女人之间的结合。《人权宣言》第16.1条原文是这样说的：

> 成年男女，不受种族、国籍或宗教的限制，有权结婚和建立家庭。他们在结婚、结婚期间和离婚时都享有平等的权利。

这是对人权混沌解释的一个很好的例子，在世界上最"民主"的国家之一，被用来服务于政治（和宗教）目的。

跨文化与人权霸权：带来问题的超国家行动

2015年3月，负责促进、培训人权和公民教育以及制定相关教学材料的政府间组织——欧洲理事会（Council of Europe），声称他们正在制定一个"定义和衡量民主能力的普遍而客观的评价体系"。有趣的是，我从该机构发来的信息中发现，"民主能力"和"跨文化能力"在交替使用。该机构定义了20项核心"民主"能力：（除其他外）责任感、包容、冲突解决能力、倾听能力、语言和沟通能力、批判性思维、同理心和开放性以及自主学习能力。同时，对每种能力的描述包括了人们应知道什么、理解什么、做到什么和不做什么。据该机构教育部的负责人说，这样做是为了测量每项能力的达到程度，并"将其纳入整个欧洲和其他地区的教师培训计划、招聘考试和学校课程”中。虽然在这些能力描述中找不到“人权”这个词，但它其实隐含在许多方面（民主、容忍、责任等等）。当然，这一行动是在特定的背景下进行的：极端主义势力在多方抬头；人们质疑自己的身份和从属地，经常通过划清自己和他人的界限以保护自己；世界面临着可怕的难民危机等。因此，人们很可能觉得欧洲理事会的这项工作非常必要，受到大家的欢迎。然而，阅读这项行动的描述时，我对其假设的“普遍”和“客观”感到担忧。谁有最终的决定权？比如决定什么是“批判性思维”，什么是“责任感”？这些能力描述代表的是谁的声音？这样做是否会导致“中心”（欧洲）对世界其他地区发号施令，规定他们什么是民主和跨文化能力？我还发现，许多和人权论述有关的部分都存在很大的问题。例如，许多跨文化学者批评了宽容的概念，因为这个词在某些地区含有贬义，并且带有“高人一等”的意味（见Dobbernack和Modood，2013；Adcock 2013年关于印度的例子）。“开放性”这一概念也是如此：哪些人可以被视为真正的“开放”？向什么“开放”？“开放性”总被认为是名副其实的吗？

2010年世界文化多样性促进对话和发展日上，发表了一篇有趣但含糊的声明，表达了联合国专家组的观点：人权是开展“有效”跨文化对话必不可少的“工具”。该声明对“文化多样性”做了多次强调，这一拟人化的词语隐藏了参与对话的社会存在，并试图消除他们的综合能力。例如，声明一开始就谈到全球化“侵蚀了文化多样性”，需要“保持文化多样性”。然而，我同意Wood（2003：21）的观点：“我们沉醉于这样一种观点，即每一个民族习俗的差异、每一个外国或地区的口音、每一个传统食谱和每一个群体态度都代表着一种独特的世界观。”该声明所倡导的文化多样性类似于博物馆中被“保护”的文物，很容易被当作“捏造的多样性”，即“把世界想象成划分得很清楚的社会群体，每个群体都有属于自己的繁荣文化传统”（Wood，2003：37）。有趣的是该声明作者的解释和声明本身是自相矛盾的：

> 文化权利包括对“文化”现存对象提出质疑的权利、选择加入或退出特定文化实体的权利以及不断创造新文化的权利。个人拥有多重的多元身份，属于不同的多元群体。因此，促进文化多样性是保护正在进行中的过程，是有利于当代和未来的可再生宝藏，保证每个人的人权是不断适应培养表达、创造和创新能力的过程。（联合国，2010）

这说明作者认为文化是不断变化的过程，承认人们有选择退出文化的权利。当提到促进文化多样性时，使用“保护正在进行中的过程、可再生的宝藏”这样的矛盾修辞法（两个相互矛盾的术语并用），很好地解释了这一过程。另外，该声明还在此主张，人权是一个直接依赖于文化表达、创造和创新的过程。我同意这些观点。然而，令人遗憾的是，该声明仅用模糊的文化一词来讨论人权与跨文化对话之间的联系。Jahoda（2012：300）正确地提醒了我们，“‘文化’不是一件事，而是一种模糊地指向一系列极为复杂现象的社会建构”。也许更重要的是，Holliday（2010：4）认为，“如果完全根据人们所处的文化去定义和限制个人的行为，那么刻板印象就成为了他们的本质，这样的话，文化将很容易导致本质主义”。这就引出了以下问题：当人们谈论与人权相关的文化时，是指谁的文化？应该尊重谁的文化，为什么？这些讨论中包含和排除了谁的声音？在处理这些问题时，交叉考虑文化和他的身份标记（性别、社会阶层、语言等），变得越来越重要。

该声明还强调了跨文化对话中使用人权的政治方面：

> 任何人不得以文化多样性作为借口，去侵犯国际法所保障的人权，限制人权的范围，也不应利用文化多样性来支持种族隔离和有害的传统惯例，尤其当这些行为本质上是为了将与人权的普遍性、不可分割性和相互依存性背道而驰的各种差异合法化。（联合国，2010）

这是跨文化性极其重要的一方面，我们将此问题归纳为：文化（或声明中的文化多样性）通常被用作“借口”和“托辞”，来歧视排斥他人并将自己置于圣坛之上。（Dervin和Machart，2015）有趣的是，这些做法在芬兰教育中非常普遍，比如芬兰教育中的他者经常被区别对待，分隔开来，被要求做一个“文化”另类，以取悦教师、教师的教育者和决策者对多元文化主义的期望。（Riitaoja，2013）对我而言，通过该声明，这就可以理解为对人权的侵犯：根据肤色和表面的差异，而不是根据芬兰出生、生活和学习这样的潜在共性，老师经常在这些学生身上犯“挑剔”的错误。

在跨文化教育中处理人权的“脆弱性”

我同意De Sousa Santos（2009：17）的观点，即我们不应抛弃人权。正如社会学家的建议，我们需要做的是想办法让人们意识到人权“目前的脆弱性”，帮助他们构建“强大的抵抗思想和实践”（De Sousa Santos，2009），并解构“跨文化”讨论和人权霸权话语的灌输形式。

接下来我会提出一些建议。正如Mchangama和Verdirame（2014）的正确主张，首先我们需要缩小范围，给人权下一个更清晰的定义。历时性地去研究世界不同地区的人权是如何被提出和建构的，这对学生来说是非常必要的。这些不同的模式之间有什么异同？在国际上哪种提法看上去更胜一筹？他们想要保留和可能应用到学校中的人权，哪些方面是以前就有的，哪些是从世界不同地区来的？关于人权的讨论被包含在学校许多科目中，并且经常在教科书中可以找到。对于老师和学生来说，考查和比较人权在不同学科中是如何被介绍和讨论的，这一点非常重要。

质疑人权的不稳定及其在跨文化对话中的人为操纵也是一个重要的教育目标。正如De Sousa Santos所说，我们需要增强“对人权的怀疑”，尤其是它们与“西方自由主义矩阵”的关系（2009；2015）。De Sousa Santos建议，应该将西方话语体系中的人权，与那些在西方看来“天生在伦理和政治方面就不如”他们的其他“人类尊严的语法”相比较（2015：3）。人权讨论中包括了哪些人，排除了哪些人？“人的尊严”在其他地方是如何被定义的？“我们的”定义方式与“他们的”定义方式有什么异同？人权越来越个人主义化这一事实也应该引起我们的充分重视（De Sousa Santos，2015：xiv）。

在更微观的层面上，让学生反思自己环境中的跨文化性和人权是很有趣的。一个有趣的点是讨论班上“少数群体”的权利（移民背景的学生、宗教代表和性少数群体等等）。继Amselle（2010：79）之后，人们可以反思一下，例如，移民背景的学生是否有权选择和/或摆脱种族、语言和文化身份的权利，在学校中，这些身份往往是强加在他们身上的。学生应有权保持或拒绝其“出身”（De Singly，2003：58）。但是在某一所学校中这些发生了多少？学校是怎么做的？人们如何才能够被赋予质疑这些行为的权利？

环境问题在人权和“跨文化”的讨论中也经常被忽略。Quessada（2013：277）提出了一个有趣的观点，就是将关注点从人类的权利转移到人类的职责。这打开了跨文化的思路。越来越多的科学家认为，我们的时代是人类纪时代（anthropocene，anthopos =人类；cene =新的或最近的），指的是人类对地球的地质和生态产生着重大而深远的影响。它标志着全新世的结束，结束了人类殖民新领土的时代（Quessada，2013）。人类纪时代的特征是人口激增，化石燃料的大量使用，对淡水的需求，生态环境的破坏以及物种的急剧灭绝，这些证据证明“人类在塑造地球地质和地理环境中起着核心作用”。在日常媒体和跨文化话语中，人们经常试图“责备”和“羞辱”最大的环境污染者，但是人类纪时代告诉我们，每个人都应该对地球历史的新篇章负责，是所有人类共同构成了一股地质的力量（Quessada，2013：274）。污染因此变成相互关联的：“我的消费方式、我的生活方式、我存在于世的事实，都在相互关联的污染面前将我与其他人联系起来。”（Quessada，2013）在环境问题面前，所有人都是平等的（2013：276）。因此，非常重要的一点是，跨文化教育必须注重这一方面，帮助学生用批判的眼光去考查关于“污染者”和“污染受害者”的话语，以及媒体关于污染超越国界的报道，更加严格地检视自己的立场和矛盾冲突（日常生活中我的消费方式是如何对周遭的环境，以及数千英里以外的环境造成直接和间接污染的？）。

反霸权方式的反思

本章回顾了跨文化与教育中的人权话语之间的联系，反思了在这些问题上存在的霸权主义的观点，并提出了“跨文化”中解决人权问题的“反霸权方法”。受Hoskins和Sallah（2011）关于跨文化能力概念批判性讨论的启发，作为本书最后两个章节的导论，我希望通过列举在教育中能够实施的关于人权和跨文化的知识、意识、理解与批判性思维，总结本章的主要观点：

1.知道某个人自己的情境中人权被侵犯或助长人权侵犯的行为。在讨论其他情况时要表现出谦卑。

2.知道跨时空的人权话语，以及其中某些话语如何保留并“统治”其他话语。从媒体和政策制定者的角度去质疑欧洲中心主义和灌输（indoctrination教育？）。

3.知道世界各地区与人权主义相对的，对“尊严”进行概念化的其他方式。讨论他们的利与弊、异与同。

4.有能力去选择和讨论人权的某些确切方面，而不是采用更全球化的方法。探知文化话语和固定身份是如何侵犯他人人权的。

5.意识到并理解人权的“脆弱性”。

6.有能力去支持那些需要选择和/或退出固定身份的人。给他们话语权。

7.批判地思考某些人对他人的自我信念和行为。

8.知道人类纪时代的特征。就自己和他人的人类职责展开讨论。

问题

1.请用你自己的话给人权下定义。

2.您认为人类与跨文化有关的职责有哪些？

3.如果我说白人老师他者化黑人学生是侵犯了学生的人权，您认为过分吗？请阐释你的观点。

4.您认为自己“思想开放”吗？“思想开放”是什么意思？

5.举例说明人们是如何用人权作为借口的。

参考文献

ADCOCK C. S. The limits of tolerance：Indian secularism and the politics of religious freedom [M]. Oxford：Oxford University Press，2013.

AMSELLE J. L. Rétrovolutions [M]. Paris：Stock，2010.

BEITZ C. R. The idea of human rights [M]. Oxford：Oxford University Press，2011.

DE SINGLY F. Libres ensemble [M]. Paris：Livre de Poche，2013.

DE OLIVEIRA V. Actionable postcolonial theory in education [M]. Basingstoke：Palgrave，2011.

DE SOUSA SANTOS B. If god were a human rights activist：Human rights and the challenge of political theologies [J/OL]. Law Social Justice and Global Development Journal，2009（1）. http：//www2.warwick.ac.uk/fac/soc/law/elj/lgd/2009_1/santos/.

DE SOUSA SANTOS B. If god were a human rights activist [M]. Stanford：Stanford University Press，2015.

DERVIN F. La meilleure éducation au monde? Contre-enquête sur la Finlande [M]. Paris：L'Harmattan，2013.

DERVIN F. & MACHART R.（Eds.）. Cultural essentialism in intercultural encounters [M]. London：Palgrave，2015.

DOBBERNACK J. & MODOOD T. Tolerance，intolerance and respect

hard to accept? [M] London: Palgrave Macmillan, 2013.

FRIEDMAN E. J., CLARK A. M., & HOCHSTELLER K. Sovereignty, democracy and global civil society: State-society relations at the UN world conferences [M]. Albany: State University of New York Press, 2005.

HAMELINK C. J. International communication: Global market and morality [M]// A. MOHAMMADI (Ed.) . International communication and globalization. London/Thousand Oaks/New Delhi: Sage, 1997.

HOLLIDAY A. Intercultural communication and ideology [M]. London: Sage, 2010.

HOSKINS B. & SALLAH M. Developing intercultural competence in Europe: The challenges [J]. Language and Intercultural Communication, 2011, 11 (2) : 113–125.

JAHODA G. Critical refl ections on some recent defi nitions of "culture" [J]. Culture & Psychology, 2012, 18: 289–303.

LEVINE R. A. & CAMPBELL D. T. Ethnocentrism: Theories of confl ict, ethnic attitudes, and group behavior [M]. New York: Wiley, 1972.

MCHANGAMA J. & VERDIRAME G. The danger of human rights proliferation: When defending liberty, less is more [J/OL]. Foreign Affairs, 2014. https: //www.foreignaffairs.com/articles/europe/2013-07-24/danger-human-rights-proliferation?page=show.

MITCHELL T. C. Biblical archeology: Documents from the British Museum [M] . London: Cambridge University Press, 1988.

QUESSADA D. L' inséparé. Essai sur le monde sans Autre [M]. Paris: PUF, 2013.

Riitaoja A. L. Toiseuksien rakentuminen koulussa：Tutkimus opetussuunnitelmista ja kahden helsinkiläisen alakoulun arjesta [M]. Helsinki：Helsingin Yliopisto，2013.

STARKEY H. Intercultural competence and education for democratic citizenship：Implications for language teaching methodology [M]// M. BYRAM（Ed.）. Intercultural competence Strasbourg：Council of Europe，2003.

UN. Statement by experts on World Day for Cultural Diversity for Dialogue & Development [EB/OL].（2010-05-21）http：//www.wluml.org/node/6325.

WOOD P. Diversity：The invention of a concept [M]. San Francisco：Encounter Books，2003.

第六章　变革的工具

——动态、现实的跨文化能力

摘　要：本章介绍了跨文化能力的复杂概念。作者呼吁对这一概念进行动态定义，质疑关于此概念的各种普遍和客观的假设。对最流行的跨文化能力模型进行了回顾和解构。然后作者建议把注意力集中到他称之为跨文化能力（复数形式）的现实方法上，这将推动从业者、研究人员和决策者修改他们对这一概念的使用。本章的结尾是对教师跨文化能力的观察，相关研究是由接受了跨文化能力培训的实习教师在实习期间完成的。

本节提出，前几节对跨文化性进行解构后，再进行跨文化性的重构。通过举例来定义和说明一系列概念工具和方法工具。有了这些工具，教育中的跨文化性会产生新的意义。在本章中，讨论了跨文化能力这一核心但存有疑义的概念。批判性地回顾了这一概念，并证明它导致了前几部分所提出的问题后，跨文化能力这个会带来问题的概念被跨文化动态的观点所替代。此外，跨文化动态的组成部分将举例说明。

以动态能力为目标

处理跨文化能力之前，让我总结一下目前为止提出的要点。有一件事是肯定的：我们需要远离这样一种观点——它强调“目标文化”的事实，它提出“文化语法”（能做的和不能做的），它重点关注文化差异，它与不同文化和文明对峙（Valette，1986）。

也许跨文化性最重要的方面是它必须通过与另一个人的互动产生，这对我们如何思考、行为、表现、呈现自己等等有影响。对Gallagher（2011：488）来说，在想到一个社会存在时，我们不可能不考虑他/她一直经历的动态过程。他建议我们时刻谨记，当我们遇到某人时，“自我中的他者”和“他人中的自我”就会出现（2011：492）。Shi-xu（2001：280）也提出了类似的主张，他批评了通常采用的“个人知识思维的方式”来处理跨文化性，这种方式完全忽略了互动是共同建构的事实。这就是为什么按照这些跨文化动态行事和考查需要政治手段，一种非常强调权力（阶序人如何定位自己和他人？）、非固化身份认同和“脸面工作”（facework）的手段，也就是说，我们如何在互动交流中保护自己和他人？（Bensa，2010；Lakoff，1990）

我将通过下面的摘录证明这些观点。几年前，芬兰一家电视频道播出了一名假日本记者的系列采访（Noriko Show）。这位记者实际上是一位著名的芬兰女演员。她伪装成一个“典型的”日本人，说着蹩脚的英语，做着傻事。其中一集里，她遇到了芬兰歌手丹尼，丹尼和其他客人一样，被她的英语和语无伦次的话语给搞糊涂了。采访进行到一半时，Noriko（记者）开始胡扯一个想象中的芬兰歌手。以下是摘录的台词：

N（Noriko）：…… 所以还有另一位芬兰歌手叫鸭达？

D（丹尼）：（沉默）…… 不好意思，你刚刚说什么？

N：还有一位芬兰歌手叫鸭达？

D：是的，我们有 ……

N：因为我昨天遇到了他，鸭达，迪迪·鸭达先生，姓鸭达，你认识他吗？

D：是的，我认识他，嗯 …… 我想我在日本的时候也有机会进入一家表演学院，他们带我去了一家表演学院，在那里他们排练了各种动作等等。

N：你知道一些功夫斗士吗？

D：是的，我很了解你们的文化，因为你们的文化太古老了，很多文化都是以你们的文化为基础的。

在这段节选中，在记者不可理喻的反应面前，客人试图挽回面子。这里有一种力量的不平衡：这位歌手认为他将出现在日本电视上，所以他需要保持形象，确保他的“脸面”是在正面的聚光灯下。正因为如此，他试图像一切正常一样继续对话，甚至称赞日本文化（“你们的文化”）是古老的，是许多其他文化的基础。这种以文化为借口的论述，使他得以摆脱虚构的歌手鸭达的纠缠，并迎合他想象中的观众。虽然这个场景中一方的对话者（Noriko）是纯虚构的，但芬兰歌手仍因正在经受的“跨文化”压力，而掉进了本质主义和文化主义的陷阱。这段摘录之前，这位歌手曾几次试图想要澄清，但最终决定不理会记者，继续自己的讨论。很明显，这次（被操纵的）采访使人想起了许多“真正的”跨文化接触，也让人明白跨文化性并不是个公式，不会有人指导你去如何运用它。

反对“普遍的”和“客观的”定义

2015年3月，欧洲理事会教育主管部门（欧洲和世界上颇具影响力的教育机构）发布的信息中提到，欧洲理事会雄心勃勃的“能够改革我们生活和工作方式的民主能力的先锋性工作”计划已被披露。作为提醒，在这条信息中，标题中的民主能力与跨文化能力放在一起，被定义为“使我们能够有效参与当今多样化民主政治的价值观、态度、技能、知识和批判性理解”。这项“先锋性工作”的目标是找到一个“普遍和客观的体系来定义和衡量（促进人权和公民教育所必需的）民主能力”。为此，“20项核心能力被挑选出来，包括责任、宽容、冲突解决、倾听技能、语言和沟通技能、批判性思维、同理心和“开放性”等，并将会测量和评价诸如“同理心”和“批判性思维”的达到程度。

Maffesoli（1976：259）认为：“对‘最好的存在方式’的追求总是通过强加‘应该是’来表达，这不可避免地导致了极权主义。”我认为，我们应该担心的是，这个预言中所包含的对“最好的存在方式”的坚持，很容易变成一个伪普遍的“应该是”。欧洲理事会提出的20项核心能力，很容易因其本身的一词多义、空洞无物以及背后隐含的欧洲中心价值观（如宽容、批判性思维、开放性等），而受到批判。其中“客观的”和“普遍的”观点也会在我们这样的后殖民世界里引发许多问题。重读这条信息，仔细思考其中关于自我和他人的有点符合常情却又略带殖民意味的话语，你会很容易产生这样的印象，即欧洲理事会正在为我称作“跨文化能力的想象工程行业”做出贡献，一个由想象和工程合成的词（Härkönen和Dervin，2015）。跨文化能力常常被欧洲理事会视为中立的信息交换与交流，而忽略了跨文化不仅包含且会助长不平衡的权力关系和差别待遇、滋生种族主义、文化主义等各种主义的事实。（见Abdallah-Pretceille，1986；Dervin，2010；Holliday，2010；Hoskins and Sallah，2011）这些都是至关重要的社会问题，需要进一步的批判性研究，以挑战当前的霸权主义、等级制度和权力差异。尽管我们生活在后现代的跨文化时代，但我却觉得欧洲委员会的建议像是在另一个时代提出的、以欧洲为中心的、普遍主义的社会政治和经济视角，并想让我们以此视角来分析世界，尽管其出发点是好的（Maffesoli，1993：8）。

在本章中，我想要证明的是，许多学者、思想家和实践者已经跳脱了诸如欧洲理事会这种“想象工程产业”，对当前教育中跨文化性的革命做出了积极贡献。他们来自各种不同的领域和子领域，用不同的视角研究跨文化：跨文化/多文化/社会正义教育、语言教育、卫生保健、商业等等。此列表尚不包括其他未在名称中体现“跨文化”一词的领域（人类学、社会学、心理学、教育的其他子领域等），倘若没有他们，“跨文化”的进化（革命）不会发生。我认为，这场进化（革命）可以帮助我们解决今天迫在眉睫的他者化、种族主义/仇外心理和社会不公等问题，并修正教育中跨文化能力的重要概念。我也对进化（革命）提出了一些意见，并对我所说的跨文化能力的“现实”手段提出了一些建议。

解构或（和）重构跨文化能力

跨文化能力的概念是教育的跨文化性中常被讨论的问题之一，尤其是教师教育、语言教育和出国留学。Spitzberg和Changnon（2009）对“市面上可见的”跨文化能力的各种模型进行了综述，并将其分为五类：（1）构成模型（Compositional models）提出列一张简单的表，包含那些看似无关的态度、技能、知识和行为;（2）共定向模型（Co-orientational models）强调交流互动以及自我与他者的建构;（3）发展模型（Developmental models）描述个体如何获得跨文化能力;（4）适应模型（Adaptational models）研究跨文化交际中人们的调整和适应;（5）因果路径模型（Causal path models）关注的是跨文化能力不同部分之间如何相互联系。

有些跨文化能力模型已在过去的几十年中“声名鹊起”，并被用在它们原来领域之外的领域。它们代表的模型基本可以归类到上述五类模型的构成模型、发展模型和适应模型中。以下三种模型不仅在我自己的情境中（芬兰教师教育），而且在世界范围内也非常有影响力，值得我们给予更多的关注和探讨。

第一个模型由 Milton J. Bennett（1986；1993）提出，被称为跨文化敏感度发展模型（The Developmental Model of Intercultural Sensitivity，DMIS）。虽然它没有被正式称为跨文化能力的模型，但它经常被这样使用（Hosaya，et al.，2010）。该模型概括了一个从民族中心主义（相信自己的文化是最好的）到民族相对主义（意识到所有的文化都是“好的”和“坏的”）的连续过程，在此过程中文化意识和理解不断增加，不断调整。该模型已被用于商业和跨文化交流研究以及世界各地的教育研究中。这种模型的主要问题是：用户必须付费才能使用；它基于能力的“水平”；它通常是按部就班地使用，就好像跨文化性是可以预先规划和固定不变的 —— 因此，该模型声称跨文化能力是可以获得的，而不是可以培养的。因此，该模型在某种意义上非常个人主义，因为它过于依赖一个人的“表现”，而忽略了这样一个事实，即跨文化性是由他人存在、权力差异、特定语境和文本互涉共同建构和影响的，某种程度上甚至是由这些因素决定的。不容忽视的是，不同的表征、情境和话语之间都会有对话，正是这些影响了一个人的行为和态度。最后，该模型在很大程度上坚持文化在连续过程中的“力量”，依赖于对不同文化知识的积累，而这些文化知识经常被用作“民族”知识的同义词（McSweeney，2012）。

接下来两个模型是在谷歌学术搜索中最受欢迎的模型。第二种模型与前一种模型有一些共同的特点。Byram（1997）认为跨文化交流能力从语言教育领域产生，起源于Hymes的交际研究。该模型是将与个人相关的知识、技能和态度等认知和动机要素进行理论化。虽然这个模型有一些有趣的特点，但我一直对它有些幼稚和实证主义的方法持批评态度（德文，2010）。例如，模型的组成部分——自我认知（savoir être）具有误导性，很容易导致沾沾自喜。它包括表现出好奇心和开放性，以及随时准备中止对其他文化的怀疑和对自己文化的信仰。对我来说，光表现是不够的，而且非常不稳定（就算我不相信我表现的东西，我仍然可以表现出来）。我们还需要质疑个体对自己和他人的态度，以及在此态度上做出的行为。另一个组成部分——知识（savoirs），指的是社会群体在自己的国家和对话者的国家的产物和实践的知识。对“国家”和“文化”的强调再次人为地划定了边界，在我们这样一个全球本土化的世界里，人们可能会对此提出怀疑（Appadurai，1996）。Byram的模型还包括另一组成部分，即批判性文化意识和/或政治教育（savoir s’engager）。这涉及跨文化公民的概念，是在Byram为欧洲理事会所做研究的框架中发展起来的。虽然这一点很有意思，但人们还是会对其背后的欧洲政治偏见、康德的道德理性观和西方的人权激进主义倾向提出批评（Matsuo，2012；参见Hoff，2014和第五章）。

最后一个极具影响力的跨文化能力模型是Darla Deardorff提出的。基于对上述“西方”能力模型的综述研究，Deardorff提出了跨文化能力金字塔模型（Pyramid Model of Intercultural Competence；2006；2009）。与Bennett和 Byram的模型一样，金字塔模型是建立在知识、技能和态度的基础上的，其组成部分也有很多问题。知识包括文化自我意识，对文化的深刻理解和认识，以及特定的文化信息。技能的基础是倾听、观察、解读、分析、评估和联系。必要的态度包括尊重（重视其他文化、文化多样性）、开放性（对跨文化学习和来自其他文化的人持开放态度，不作评论）以及好奇心和探索心（容忍模棱两可和不确定性）。Deardorff列出了他所期待的结果:（所期待的外部结果；基于跨文化知识、技能和态度）进行有效恰当的表现和沟通，以在一定程度上实现自己的目标;（期望的内部结果）信息参考框架/过滤转换：适应性（适应不同的沟通风格和行为；适应新的文化环境）；灵活性（选择和使用适当的沟通方式和行为；认知灵活性）；民族关联视角；同理心。如果这些方面没有被解构，它们就会很容易保持高度的本质主义和非批判性。

再回到Spitzberg和Changnon（2009）的观点，我们注意到在这三个模型中，共定向模型和因果路径模型往往是缺乏的；也就是说，重点是个体的表现，而不是他们构成的互动或关系。例如，期待的结果“有效恰当的表现和沟通”往往带有偏见。在教育中，谁能决定什么是有效和恰当的跨文化，特别是当这些是共同构建和协定的时候？在这三个模型中，重点还包括态度、技能、知识和行为。这些要素有的会带来问题，有的要素的“习得”非常困难或不可评估。例如，同理心、灵活性、“视角”等等。由于我们需要依靠话语和/或行动来检验这些要素，所以我们只能关注它们的实施。

构建跨文化能力的方法

首先，我同意P. Nynas（2001：34）的观点，他认为“我们不可能提供成功的沟通技巧或跨文化沟通的因果模型”。我们甚至可以更进一步，与哲学家亨利·柏格森（1907：72）争辩他的观点同向：“试图给生活分配一个目标，即人类意义上的目标，是徒劳的。谈论目标就像是想到一个预先存在的模型，我们要做的只是去实现它。”

前一节提到的三种模型，虽然在某些教育背景下仍然适用，但依然值得质疑。它们象征着一个时代的“跨文化性”研究和实践，与反对他者化、反对霸权、反对等级制度和权力差异等教育的核心目标并不相符。接下来，我提出对研究和教学中构建跨文化能力的方法进行元分析：“固态的”雅鲁斯式的、“液态的”理想主义的和“液态的”现实主义的分析方法。这些分类是在密切观察和分析教育和交流领域现有的跨文化能力的关键方法后提出的。已经有很多发表的文章对跨文化能力的“固态”方法进行了批评，而前一节中对三种模型的评论也暴露了一些意见。“流动的”类别代表了跨文化的进化（革命），批判性地反思了上述问题。“固态”和“液态”的比喻直接借用自社会学家Zygmunt Bauman，他把我们的世界描述为“液态的”（有些人会说是后现代的），与现代民族国家的“固体性”相对（Bauman，2004）。

跨文化能力“固态的”方法是根据国家文化或语言将个人分门别类，分配静态的身份。为了说明这种方法，我使用了欧洲理事会（一个对欧洲和世界教育都有影响力的欧洲机构）的一份出版物，该出版物是基于“教师教育跨文化交流培训”项目。《发展和评估跨文化沟通能力：语言教师和教师教育者的指南》一书于2007年出版，之后一直被该机构使用，最近一次是应用于2015年的项目中。研究团队遵循Byram的模式设定学习目标：学习各种文化，习得一种文化，在两种或两种以上的文化之间进行调解。书中没有提及诸如霸权、等级制度和权力差别等紧迫问题。因此，作者巧妙地将世界分为文化局内人和文化局外人。最终的结果是，跨文化交际就像板块运动相互碰撞。用更科学的术语来说，就是用本质主义和文化主义的概念来描述这个很成问题的观点，即在跨文化交流中祛除人们的综合能力，并将问题“归咎于”他们的文化（见Holliday，2010；Frenkiel和Rocca，2013）。此外，过分强调差异（而不是差异性和相似性的综合体，见第二章）会导致跨文化能力的固化。E. Said（1978：349）认为，“文化和文明是如此相互联系和相互依存，以至于无法用统一或简单的语言来描述它们的个体性”。因此，在我们这样一个相互关联的世界里，文化和所谓的文化群体之间的界限是相当模糊的（Subrahmanyam，2011）。分离了文化，这种跨文化能力模型就与前文提到的亨廷顿的（1996）“文明冲突”思想相对应。

第二种方法叫作雅鲁斯法（Janusian），它倾向于在前一种方法（“分门别类”）和后现代的合作建构主义的方法之间摇摆不定，后者是在所有因素中首要考虑身份定位和文化话语的不稳定性。这种摇摆不定常常导致人们在解释、分析和构建跨文化交际时的矛盾和不一致，导致特权和权力差异。大多数时候，“雅鲁斯主义者”没有意识到这些问题，也没有意识到他们从一个立场转向另一个立场的事实。其中一些问题已在《发展和评估跨文化交际能力：语言教师和教师教育者的指南》中指出。例如在此书开篇，作者声称“全球范围内的沟通和新技术的发展创造了跨国的文化”或“我们知道语言教师通过各种信息来源向我们展示具有代表性的文化：教学大纲、教材、文本的选择和他们自己的经历”。然而，他们同时声称："跨文化的有效交流"意味着人们应该根据相互尊重、互惠互利的文化的特殊性特征和一般性特征，完成人与人之间的谈判。"文化特殊性"和"文化一般性特征"的提法似乎与"跨国文化"的概念相矛盾，与前文引用中对语言教师的批评相矛盾。正如Abdallah-Pretceille（1986）所言，我相信任何提及文化的地方都是一种代表。雅鲁斯主义代表了潜在的危险立场，如果一个人没有注意并承认这些矛盾，这些矛盾就会总是影响无力保护自己的"底层人民"。

接下来的两个观点都属于"跨文化能力的液态方法"类别，符合当前对后现代和后殖民时代教育现实的分析，与对前两种教育方法的批评相一致。例如，Van Dijk（1987）等人认为，这些方法证明了跨文化能力是如何导致偏见的传播、复制和逆来顺受。Adrian Holliday（2010）补充说，它还含蓄地表达了"隐藏的一对概念——优越感和自卑感"（Van Dijk，1987：386）。类似地，后殖民时代的教育民族主义者Vanessa Andreotti（2011）从主流的西方认识论中看到了跨文化能力研究对"他者"的敌意，而这种认识论正是基于欧洲启蒙主义运动。在她对英国教育政策和实践的分析中，Andreotti（2011）表明"他者"经常被用来证明"我们"的优越性。我认为跨文化能力的固态模型也有类似的问题（Dervin，2011）。

第一种模型被称作（液态）理想主义的，第二种模型称作（液态）现实主义的。（液态）理想主义方法一直是跨文化性和跨文化能力批判性讨论的重点，至少已有10年之久（见Piller，2011）。它的出发点是多元多样性观点（每个人都是多样的，不管他们的出身、肤色、社会背景等）。它的目的是告诉我们非本质主义、非文化主义思想的危险性，并"压制"它们，因为它们会掩盖歧视性、权力性和优越性的话语，很容易地被当作借口和托辞（Dervin，2015）。这种（液态）理想主义方法也质疑"固化的”起源问题（参见Dervin，2015），“固化的”起源会掩盖导致（隐藏的）歧视、压迫、不公和等级制度的“密码”。

多年来，我一直是液态“理想主义”方法的支持者。然而，现在我用意识形态的视角看到了一个问题：它倾向于忽略这样一个事实，即它本身是带有意识形态的（像其他方法一样），因为它致力于不可能达到的非本质主义和非文化主义的目标。这些目标当然是崇高的，在跨文化教育中应始终铭记。然而，它们可能非常不稳定，因为它们是在与“复杂”人类的沟通交流和特定背景下商定而成的，对权力关系有一定影响。在某些情况下，因为一个人感到自卑或仅仅因为他累了，即使他很努力，也无法实现这些崇高的目标。另一个问题关系到这样一个事实，即（液态）理想主义方法没有完全认识到（像其他方法一样）它制造了跨文化能力的新想象工程，这不仅会导致沾沾自喜，还会导致居高临下的态度（“我是非本质主义者，而你不是”）。如果我认为我是非本质主义者（我不可能真的是），这是否意味着我“赢得了战斗”？此外，（液态）理想主义方法多少有些令人沮丧。非本质主义是无法实现的理想：例如，当学生被迫相信理想有尽头时，他们如何用这种方法应对持久的斗争？他们如何应对这种挫败感？

对于跨文化能力的（液态）现实主义方法，我建议应该充分考虑超越这个棘手问题的愿望，认识到本质主义是一种“普遍的罪恶”，没有人是免疫的。虽然这看起来令人失望，但这种方法承认“陈词滥调；常备词语；遵守传统的、标准化的表达和行为准则，具有社会公认的保护我们不受现实伤害的功能”（Arendt，1978：4）。该方法确实承认了非本质主义和非文化主义的重要性，但同时敦促其支持者保持对任何互动行为的“简单复杂性”的意识。“简单复杂性”是一个由简单和复杂两个词组合而成的词，它代表了简单和复杂的连续统一体，而简单和复杂是我们必须时刻面对的两个过程（Dervin，2015）。作为研究者和实践者，我们有必要认识到并接受这一点，即我们只能在实践中简化跨文化现象。简单复杂性，是一般系统理论（General Systems Theory）、哲学、生物学和神经科学中新出现的理论（Berthoz，2012；Louie，2009），代表了每个社会人每天都要面对的经验连续体。我们与他人交流时，都需要在简单和复杂的想法和观点之间来回切换。这意味着我们最后经常会反驳自己，不确定自己在想什么，根据特定情景和对话者调整我们的话语，用“善意的谎言”取悦对方，等等。有时我们说的话显示出一定程度的复杂性（例如，“我相信每个人都有多种身份”或“我不相信刻板印象”），也会迅速回归简单（“但我认为芬兰人是这样或那样的”）。因此，既不可能完全达到简单性，也不可能完全达到复杂性，看似简单的东西也可能变得复杂，反之亦然。在过去的几十年里，复杂性在大多数研究领域得到了普及。世界是复杂的；人是复杂的。然而，我们这些复杂的人（研究人员、实践者、决策者）能够看透复杂性吗？我们自身的复杂性使得我们不可能理解他人的复杂性。没有人能声称自己能够从复杂的角度分析、理解和/或谈论跨文化性，因为迟早复杂会变成简单，简单会变成复杂。将跨文化能力“简单复杂化”在于，认识和承认一个人虽然无法接触其复杂性，但可以在“简单”和“复杂”之间相互切换，就像西西弗斯推着巨石上山一样。从某种意义上说，（液态）现实主义方法类似于前面介绍的雅鲁斯方法，只是人们意识到了这种方法的缺点。此外，与雅鲁斯主义不同的是，（液态）现实主义方法试图尽可能多地将立场拉向简单复杂性的复杂一面，同时考虑到不回到简单是不可能达成简单复杂性的。这么做当然会让我们感到不安和眩晕。

下表总结了跨文化能力的四种不同类别。

方法	“固态”	雅鲁斯	（液态）理想主义	（液态）现实主义
成分	分门别类 基于非批评主义、个人主义和刻板印象因素的不可思议的配方 对差异的过度强调	分门别类 建构主义	跨文化性是带有意识形态的（未能认识到这一观点也是带有意识形态的） 相信彻底的改变 失败是不可接受的	跨文化性总是带有意识形态的，即使从这个角度看 简单复杂性（简单和复杂的连续统一体） 接受失败和成功
影响	本质主义 文化主义 等级层次 不公平	矛盾 隐含的不公平和不一致	理想主义的定位沮丧的感觉	失望和“眩晕” 可以看作跨文化的悲观方法

跨文化能力的现实主义方法

在本节中，我感兴趣的是（液态）现实视角如何处理跨文化能力。首先，它应该超越程式化和“食谱式”的跨文化能力。跨文化能力开发和/或习得的简单进展（“阶段”）是被拒绝的。（液态）现实主义观点认为，和其他社会现象一样，跨文化能力是由矛盾体、不稳定性和不连续性组成的，它的主要目标是“适应人类生活的起起伏伏”（Bergson，1934）。具体而言，这意味着避免“对思想和存在形成固定依赖”（Bergson，1934），将不稳定性置于所有跨文化活动的中心：身份的不稳定性、文化话语的不稳定性、权力关系的不稳定性、对彼此感情的不稳定性等等。根据Lifton的观点（1993：1），即使我们“从小学习的都是恒常性和稳定性”，我们也要“异常迅速地适应社会文化和经济世界的不一致性和不可预测性”。认识到不稳定性可以进一步帮助我们认识到，这个世界特别是我们自己和他人，既不是被编写好的程序，也没有谁比谁更好，我们应该修正人与人之间的权力关系。

另一个关系到跨文化能力的重要问题是，要适应不舒适感，敢于踏入危险区域，并在处理跨文化交际时接受某种程度的“痛苦”。当前的“跨文化能力想象工程产业”常常希望通过制造“正确的跨文化”情境和/或教育内容来保护个体不受上述现象的影响，却让他们回避并分散了他们对结构性不平等、压迫和新形式种族隔离的注意力。因此，我们需要创造新的跨文化交际情境，帮助学生测试他们对不舒适感和挫败感的抵抗能力，学会举一反三。

由于跨文化能力的（液态）现实主义方法对有缺陷的文化概念采取了批判的立场，目前广泛公认最需要做的是对跨文化能力相关研究的交叉分析（Collins，2009）。因此，除关注常常受到指责的文化、种族或种族框架外，社会经济视角、政治历史视角也一样受到重视。交叉分析致力于考察社会标签和“生物”标签/身份标记，比如语言、种族、民族、阶级、性别、宗教等标记之间相互关联的本质（柯林斯，2009），尤其是当这些因素被结合在一起时，它们是否导致不公正、不平等、歧视和不利地位。根据Hoskins和Sallah（2011：114）的研究，跨文化能力的研究往往忽略了这些方面，而只关注文化差异“比较容易研究”和“无关政治”的方面。交叉分析可以帮助我们在跨文化的语境中讨论更广泛的结构力量，比如“资本主义、种族主义、殖民主义和性别歧视”（Hoskins和Sallah，2011），帮助我们以多方位视角考察权力差异的影响，帮助我们对跨文化交际进行“个性化”分析，而不仅是根据文化/民族身份一概而论。最后，这还可以让跨文化学习者融入更多的政治视角，把对他们而言重要的“斗争”（如妇女的权利）和不那么重要的方面（如种族、语言）进行交叉研究。

我在其他地方注意到，大多数跨文化能力模型往往过于个人主义，因此缺乏对话视角（Dervin，2011）。而（液态）现实主义视角却将这个方面考虑在内。跨文化能力是由不同个体在特定环境中共同构建的，这意味着对话需要成为所有跨文化能力方法的中心。对于Shi-xu（2001：290）来说，误解、不理解、沟通障碍等都是“共同导致、共同带来的影响。任何个人、团体、民族、文化、地区等都不可能单独对某件事负责，也不可能取得最大可能的成功”。社会学家M. Maffesoli（1993）提出的“集体自我”的观点对反击这一重大缺陷非常有用。杜绝这种个人主义的观点后，我们就可以在跨文化发生时，审视我和他人之间的相互依赖关系。不同自我之间的对话在跨文化交流中也很重要。对于Watkins（2000：2）来说，自我是“不同角色（或‘自我和对象的表征’）的集合，这些角色充满了一个人的思想、感受和行动。换句话说，自我是一个角色世界，有的角色去取悦别人，有的去获取别人的认同”。在考虑跨文化能力时，这点是非常重要的。太多的模型“指责”其中某位参与者能力不足，而她的能力却取决于另一位参与者（实际个体或虚拟个体）的存在。例如，一个人遇到一个外国人，这个外国人与他的熟人或朋友有着惊人的相似之处和相同的特征。这种“互文性”会对这些个体之间如何构建跨文化性、如何对待彼此以及如何定位自己产生影响。这就是惯用的跨文化方法的问题所在。这些方法把别人说的话（Valsiner，2002）当作他们跨文化能力的证据，却不努力去识别交流行为或个体话语中所呈现的对他者带来的影响。为了公平对待人们，集团化跨文化能力应是被优先考虑的事项，并让集团全体人员共同分担跨文化事件中的责任。作为一名研究者，这就意味着我需要在分析和解释数据时加入我自己的声音，在采访别人时检视我对眼前发生事情的影响。

（液态）现实主义方法中的另一个跨文化能力的主要原则处于跨文化交际想象工程（见Dervin，2015）的中心地位。戏谑的是，Mikhail Bakunin（1979：178）认为“所有的历史中，四分之一是现实，至少四分之三是想象”。现实主义方法认为，跨文化现象取决于游戏和梦想，这一点必须予以承认和接受。大多数“市面上”的跨文化能力模型都落入了“成功至上”的陷阱，这是我们这个时代的一个问题。我们应该换一种视角去相信和接受失败，并在某种意义上将失败作为提升未来学习和自我批评的有益方面。行为艺术家Marina Abramovic（2014）在谈到自己的艺术时，非常明确地解释了失败在跨文化能力中意味着什么：“你永远不知道实验结果会怎样。它可能是伟大的，也可能是相当糟糕的，但失败是非常重要的，因为它包括学习的过程，使你能够达到一个新的水平，并以其他方式看待你的工作。”跨文化能力经常被当作用来控制交际中发生的事情并防止失败的某种技术。但有趣的是，我们也可以从游戏公司Supercell（2013）的首席执行官那里学到一些东西。他解释到，他的战略是在两年内打造一家价值25亿英镑的公司：“你必须消除对失败的恐惧。如果一款游戏出了问题，我们会为它的开发者举办一个派对，开香槟庆祝他们从中吸取了教训。作为一家公司，我们失败的次数远多于成功。我们已经扼杀了5款游戏，只发行了2款。你需要冒险才能成功，为此你必须消除对风险的恐惧。”在这个痴迷于选择成功的世界里，和庆祝成功一样去庆祝失败，应该成为跨文化能力的“天然”组成部分。当然，重要的是要确保每个人都要面对失败，而不仅仅是少数人或那些被认为与“我们”非常不同的人。

实习教师的跨文化能力：一个例子

本节分析的数据来自为期一年的芬兰国际教师教育计划（见Dervin，2015；Dervin和Hahl，2015）。该项目每学年招收约20名新生。该项目为芬兰和其他国家的学生提供教师资格培训，将“更新的”跨文化性置于项目中心。作为课程的一部分，学生需通过讲座修习“批判的跨文化教育”，并在实习期间完成实践报告。在此之中，实践报告中包含的一个活动将为我们提供以下数据：

> 根据你在学校实习期间所经历的跨文化交流，写下五个与之相关的故事。如果这些故事与误解、冲突等有关，请解释它们是如何被化解的。

我收集了所有交上来的故事，并通读了一遍，然后把17位职前教师实习学校中涉及老师的故事放在了一边。在这85个故事中，有25个故事是关于教师的跨文化能力的（约30%）。这些教师既有芬兰人，也有外国人，因为17名职前教师大部分都在国际/芬兰学校实习。这些故事背后的基本原理是为了让我通过学生讲述这些“跨文化故事”的方式，了解学生是如何运用他们在实习前的12节课中接触到的知识、临界性和反身性的。当然，必须言明的是，以下分析的目的不是评判职前教师观察到的教师。正如我们看到的，大多数的观察结果都是负面的。我们需要记住，这些故事是选择过的，它们可能并不能反映学生在学校所经历的复杂性。此外，我们需要注意到，这项练习本身可能导致学生只选择“特殊的”而忽略了“普通的”。这些故事应该被认为是有条件的、片面的，甚至是虚构的。

教师是跨文化“智慧”的代言人

本小节是唯一对教师跨文化能力持积极看法的章节。在下面的节选中，实习学校的老师们为职前教师们树立了很好的榜样。他们的跨文化“智慧”包括帮助不同语言背景的学生，教他们临界性和如何持守后殖民主义立场。这样一来，职前教师就把这些教师描绘成“业余的跨文化主义者”（见Said，1993），他们质疑意识形态，寻求复杂性和更多的公正。前两段摘录是相似的，都是关于通过另一位语言相同的学生或国际职前教师的额外辅助，来帮助有需要的学生。

（学生1姓名）来自（国家），就读于（芬兰学校名称）。

（学生2姓名）是芬兰人，但是他（和前一名学生在同一个国家）学习了四年，所以他会说前一名学生的语言。他们在那所学校是同班同学。数学课上老师用英语授课。如果（学生1）听不懂，那么（学生2）就尽力解释。即使是老师也鼓励（学生2）用（学生1）的语言去教她，如果他觉得（学生1）听不懂。

在第一段摘录中，这位教师被描述为依靠一名芬兰学生作为“跨文化调解员”来支持一名移民学生，而移民学生的语言是芬兰学生会说的。这样做，老师同意修改他的角色，并为不稳定性打开大门，因为他无法“控制”两个学生用外语分享什么，必须完全依赖学生。

在下一段摘录中，一名与班上的移民学生使用同一种母语的职前学生被鼓励使用这种语言来支持该（移民）学生：

> 当我们和我的导师讨论这个问题时，她建议如果我看到他在纠结时，试着用外语和他交谈。但我不确定这是否是个好主意。在我看来，我这样做会把他单独凸显出来，考虑到他的年龄（13岁），他可能会觉得很尴尬。我的导师解释说，恰恰相反，这样做是公平的，因为她总是可以用班上其他学生的母语帮助他们，但这位移民学生却从来没有这样的机会。最后我还是在全班都在做单项练习时，过去和他说话。我没说太多，只是问他练习做得如何，但因为我是用（外语）和他说的，他吃了一惊。而且似乎是一个惊喜。

如此看来，职前教师的第一反应是怀疑。学习了跨文化讲座的课程后，她提出了一个问题，即讲一门小语种语言可能会将学生单独凸显出来。而她有经验的教师则提出了公正的论点，作为说外语的理由。令这位职前教师惊讶的是，这个策略似乎奏效了，她注意到，这个学生被他现在可以用自己的语言学习这一事实改变了。在我的课上，我们曾质疑所谓的“民族语言”在课堂上的使用，以及它们可能带来的尴尬和隔离感。在她分享的故事中，这位职前教师注意到，民族语言也可以作为增强学生信心的一种方式。通过这样的做法，她能够对讲座中提到的意识形态之一提出怀疑。

在以下的摘录中，有经验的教师对学生和职前教师的假设提出了怀疑。在第一个摘录中，老师责备学生在观察课上用法语取笑日本人。一些日本人参加了这堂课：

一个学生跟他们打招呼说:“哦!不是所有的人都懂法语。他们怎么能理解这堂课呢?”老师说:“靠数学。”男孩继续说:“所以如果我去日本,我可以理解日语教的数学课。”

老师说这要看情况,学生们开始模仿日本人说话,然后嘲笑他们。然后老师告诉他不要再胡闹了,相反,他应该学会尊重所有人,包括日本人。

在这段摘录中,这位老师不接受任何“种族主义”的霸凌,因此坚持政治立场而斥责了学生。许多学生在他们的故事中表达了疑惑,想知道在这种情况下老师应该如何表现:他们应该保持安静,开始在课堂上讨论这些事情,还是责备学生?这段摘录中老师的做法是后者。我们应该看到在某些案例中,当种族主义或仇外行为发生在课堂上时,教师的处理方式是被动的。

本节的最后一段摘录是关于一位职前教师和她的导师在国际文凭课程(IB)课堂上的一次讨论。后者建议使用的文本在职前教师看来有点多此一举,因为文本对洋娃娃一词进行了解释(贝茨娃娃和芭比娃娃),她认为这个词不言自明,无须解释:

我发现很有趣的是,那些很难但对理解文本信息有重要意义的词没有得到解释。但是像贝茨娃娃或芭比娃娃这样的词却给读者进行了解释。我认为这是很有意思的,作者选择向读者解释这些词语,因为这些文本节选自一本专门用于国际文凭课程的书。我向我的导师提出这一点,她却评论说,这是一件非常以西方为中心的事。

> 我感到有些恼怒，因为我并没有觉得自己是以西方为中心的。相反，我认为我离西方中心远着呢！……她没懂我的意思，我感到很尴尬，也许还有点恼火。我发现我的血压高得吓人。我决定不去忧虑这个评论，因为我知道我的导师当时对我不是很了解，因此，我不应该再为它烦恼了。

这位职前教师告诉我们，当她的导师指责她“以西方为中心”时，她非常强烈反对的是，“以西方为中心”是一个我们在讲座上讨论和质疑过的概念。有趣的是，职前教师并不质疑自己的话语，而是指责她的导师不理解她。但导师提出了一个重要观点，可以帮助职前教师的跨文化培训。这段摘录表明，虽然有经验的老师看起来很明智，但职前教师似乎很难反思自己的态度。

第一部分分析了职前教师所讲述的跨文化智慧行为。这些“好做法”表明职前教师能够在课堂上分辨公正、关怀和支持的态度。

教师是社会不公的推动者

社会公正的概念是职前教师跨文化培训的核心内容。许多关于教师的故事中都直接或间接提到了这个概念。这些故事包括或明或暗地单独凸显学生和教师的被动态度。第一个摘录展现了课堂上对性别的分离。故事的表达方式由于使用被动语态而变得格外有趣——老师就在那里的某处，但是间接显现着。事实上，这似乎是学校的系统问题，而不是个别老师的“错误行为”：

> 我在学校的时候，注意到男生和女生常常分开坐。课桌通常被分成三排，每个班都被分成三排，每一排要么全是男生，要么全是女生。事实上，有时座位被分成两个区域，由此班里男生坐左边一半，女孩坐右边一半。课堂上很多活动需要结对子完成，这意味着一些学生需要偶尔移动，因为他们各自的合作伙伴不在。然而，即使在这种情况下，男孩总是被要求与男孩搭档，而女孩则是与女孩搭档。

教育中的性别问题也在跨文化讲座中讨论过，“性别蒙蔽”也被当作问题讨论过。许多其他国际职前教师也记录了男孩和女孩之间的分割，并表示了他们的震惊，因为在他们的印象中芬兰是世界上性别平衡做得较好的国家之一。

在一些故事中，有经验的老师被塑造成故意单独凸显某些学生的发动机。在下面的摘录中，学生因为他们的宗教（伊斯兰教）和肤色被“拎出来”：

> 我参加的某一节课是关于言论自由的。老师提出的问题是，几年前被许多穆斯林认为侵犯了他们的丹麦著名漫画是否应该被审查。所有发言的学生都支持原则上的言论自由，除了一个学生。这唯一持保留意见的是一个小男孩，可能来自穆斯林家庭。我想，他可能在课堂上都没来得及思考和形成自己的观点，更别说有机会表达出来。他只是被多数压倒了，时间很快就到了。老师似乎没注意到这位唯一持保留意见的男孩竟没能在讨论中得到一丝发言的机会。

职前教师记录这一事件时，他显然被这种不公平的行为和潜意识的沉默所困扰，虽然这位老师可能是想“解放”并“启发”他的学生对先知漫画的兴趣，但他同时却在分裂班级，而将其中一名成员排除在外（Simmel，2013：62）。由于职前教师正好要教下一节课，他决定先让这位“穆斯林”学生发言，这样他就可以表达自己的观点。

下面的选段讲述了一个非常相似的情节，它发生在一节讨论广告的语言特征和视觉特征的课上：

> 一个广告里是一位著名的非裔美国说唱歌手和一位女模特。因为这是一个香水广告，所以他们的姿势相当露骨，却没有跨越底线。…… 这个广告带来了一系列问题，比如性冲动、男性支配和权力、女性从属和物化等，然后老师转向其中一个学生，问他对这个画面感觉如何。这个学生是个黑人，我认为这里体现了文化干预和跨文化的复杂性：好像这位黑人学生是唯一有能力 —— 或者说有特权 —— 回答老师问题的人。毕竟还有其他好几个男孩，老师本来可以要求他们回答的。我觉得这男孩感觉自己被孤立了。

又一次，一位老师转向一位“少数派”代表，询问他的意见 —— 好像他的看法可以代表其他黑人的看法。虽然职前教师不确定这位学生的反应（“我觉得这男孩感觉自己被孤立了”），他似乎认为老师本可以采取其他的行动。总之，这位职前教师认为，“有时让学生成为焦点对整个班级来说是一件好事。但是老师仍然有责任知道该问什么，什么时候问以及该问谁。这可以被看作一个转折点，标志着该学生已经开始发展与自己未来教学有关的反思性和批判性。

最后这篇摘录是有疑问的，因为职前教师不确定这一篇的后果：

我观摩了一节物理课，学生们在课堂上分组做实验。男孩（1）可能来自中东，想向另一个男孩（2）借一块橡皮，男孩（2）似乎是非裔芬兰人。男孩（2）很明白地告诉了男孩（1）他没有橡皮擦。但是男孩（1）发现男孩（2）确实有一块橡皮擦。男孩（1）说了一句“种族主义混蛋，滚回肯尼亚去”，老师要么没听见，要么无视。没有采取进一步的行动。

从最后一句话（“未采取进一步的行动”）看出，职前教师可能在分享他对于老师被动态度的惊讶。同样，许多职前教师对于自己观察到的很多教师对这类行为放任自流的事件非常惊诧。

教师能分得很清

在至少三个故事中，职前教师分享了一些事件，在这些事件中，教师明显对一些学生使用了歧视性语言。以下两段摘录展示了针对性取向和种族问题的此类做法。

在第一个摘录中，这名学生对两位老师针对两名男学生的潜在恐同言论缺乏关注表示惊讶：

在基础训练中我两次注意到两个不同的老师间接地使用同性恋的概念作为约束学生的方式。比如“你（学生1）能不能把放在他（学生2）身上的手拿开一会儿”——用带着一丝讥讽与暗示的口吻说道。另一位老师也用了这样的方式，他说：“我知道我们生活在21世纪，两个男孩手牵手是可以的，但是你能私下里这样做吗?”但是老师们并不会以这种方式对待女孩子，也许传统上人们更容易接受女孩子之间的亲近与亲密。

职前教师讲授这一事例的方式着实有趣。他使用直接引语来增加说话内容的影响力，但他也评论了这些话是如何说的（“讥讽”和“暗示”），以及这些话如何不会被用在女孩身上。通过对这些现象的解释，职前教师表现出了识别教育中歧视话语和异常/正常话语的意识。

虽然他没有对老师上述行为的后果发表评论，但人们很容易会想象到这些行为可能招致的霸凌和辱骂。

下面这段话记录了实习教师与一位老师直接讨论的结果，显示了在对他人和包法利主义（见文化部分）的欠考虑之处：

　　我一位老师说，比起外来学生，她更信赖芬兰本土的学生。她说：“我信任芬兰本土的学生，因为他们很少说谎。”我想她对外来学生知之甚少。

尽管这位老师似乎并未提及文化概念，但从这段节选中，我们可以看到某种互文性，带有“芬兰人是诚实的”这样的刻板印象和普遍表象。提到这个现象时，我对文化主义的概念提出了怀疑。根据Frenkiel和Rocca（2013：14）的观点，很明显，老师把这个论点当作建立芬兰人和他者二分法的简单方式。你也可以在这个故事中发现新种族主义迹象。同样，通过直接引用老师的话，职前教师会给读者留下一定印象。

最后一段摘录与前一位老师的说辞有一些相似之处。职前教师告诉我们，一位有着阿拉伯名字、在英国生活过的学生，曾经上过一堂课：

> 他的课堂反应比其他学生稍快一些，总是尝试着对老师进行提问。虽然老师有20年的教学经验，但他对那个学生的行为仍旧感到不舒服，并对我说，这个学生改变了整个班级的动态。

这段摘录很有趣，因为职前教师在解释老师对学生有看法之前，提到了学生的种族。职前教师是否认为学生的种族（他甚至告诉我们学生的父母是摩洛哥人）和教师的态度之间存在某种联系？考虑到这位教师的长期从教经历，但他似乎也不能理解这种联系。

最后两个小节表明，职前教师已经学会了如何在教育背景下识别跨文化和意识形态的“干扰性”话语（Holliday，2010）。Wood（2003：40）断言到：老师们似乎在观察柏拉图寓言洞穴中“人为多样性”的影子。再一次声明，这一节并不想指责教师的种族主义或对外来学生的漠视。希望通过这些故事和观察，职前教师能够对自己在类似情况下的态度和行为提出反思。

教师对教学中的跨文化内容反思不足

在跨文化课程中，我们也花时间讨论了跨文化性成为课程规划、教学内容和材料设计的重要组成部分。在一些故事中，职前教师分享了一些情节，表明教师在制订教学计划时并不总是会考虑跨文化性这个组成部分。这些例子涉及公民学、英语和物理课程。

让我们从一位公民学老师谈起。一位职前教师记录了一堂关于共产主义的课。老师让学生把身上所有的钱都放在桌子上。对于职前教师来说，这是不可接受的，因为“这很明显会让教室里的每个人都对学生的经济和社会阶层有一些了解”。她补充说，这位老师在计划上课内容时可能没有考虑到这一点。通过这个例子，职前教师表明他已经超越民族或种族，成功抓住了跨文化的要义，并且考虑到社会阶层和经济状况也会严重影响同辈和老师对学生的看法。

还有一位职前教师在说到一堂语言课时，他很疑惑为什么老师要做一个把国家比作动物、物体等的练习。有个学生说这让她感到不舒服——尤其是当别的学生选择了可能会冒犯他人的负面却有趣的词汇时。她解释道：

> 其中有一堂课上，老师给了学生一张表格去填。表格上写着这样的句子：如果芬兰是一种动物，它会是……还有：如果西班牙是一种动物，它会是……表上有很多这样的比较，学生必须想出一些代表国家的东西。我认为在某种意义上这是个有趣的练习，看看学生们是如何看待他们自己的国家和西班牙的，但同时也给出了很多刻板印象。

这名职前教师的反应是典型的“批判性的跨文化主义者”，应该受到赞扬。她甚至提出教师可以如何利用这样的练习来培养学生的跨文化能力。这个例子也再次证明，学生正在为自己未来的教学制订策略：

> 很明显，学生只能给出一个词的答案，但我认为老师可以给出

更多的解释或说：是的，这是非常正确的，但那个词怎么样？我认为谈论刻板印象和普遍表征很重要，因为这是我们开始了解一个文化或国家的方式，但我们需要更深入地去了解，并提供更多的例子，而不仅仅是第一个出现在脑海里的例子。如果我要做这个练习，我会抓住机会告诉学生，这些回答是多维的，没有唯一的正确答案。

她的建议似乎很好地呼应了研究多维性、刻板印象和普遍特征的观点。

本小节描述了芬兰一些国际职前教师的跨文化准备工作。这种准备代表了一种努力，即帮助职前教师“好整以暇，备战革命”（Bachelard，1938）。本研究的目的之一，是分析职前教师在实习期间观察有经验的教师时如何将跨文化因素考虑在内。通过分析职前教师所分享的关于教师的故事，表明他们努力在分辨“好的”和“坏的”/有疑问的做法，至少在这25个故事中是这样。虽然职前教师没有被要求为他们的解释找出理论支撑，但看来跨文化讲座中分享的一些观点和争论对他们产生了影响。我们那位“批判的多元文化主义者”展示了，职前教师们似乎已有能力意识到、认识到、推进并呈现/捍卫她/他的多元多样性和其他人的多元多样性。此外，他们似乎意识到某种“跨文化的”意识形态。当然，对他们如何将知识应用于实践的长期研究，会使这些结果更加可信。显然，上述过程是尤为重要的第一步。

这并不是批评有经验的教师缺乏跨文化能力，而是要看职前教师能否通过观察他们未来的教师职业，识别他们可能想要另作处理的现象，或至少是去面对和/或讨论。某些职前教师甚至能够提出替代方案，而不仅仅是对发生的情况和对学生的影响进行描述。

参与这项研究的所有学生都是外国人，大多数人不会说芬兰语。他们将来在芬兰当外教可能会觉得不舒服，所以他们在实习期间能够反思这一特点非常重要。一些职前教师已经注意到，在教育背景下芬兰人和非芬兰人并不总是公平对待彼此的。例如，一位职前教师解释说："当不愉快发生时，非芬兰籍的教师就会提到芬兰和糟糕的天气或不合群的人，这是非常不合适的。但是，芬兰教师也会对外国人持有刻板印象，比如美国教师不爱干净，英国教师很懒散。"通过反思各方话语的不一致性和不稳定性，通过避免偏袒任何一方，职前教师也许能够摆脱这种歧视性的和可能造成伤害的话语。

在这些故事当中，职前教师们并未过多地提及他们在观察经验丰富的教师时所感到的不适。但在口头上，许多人在目睹某些歧视行为或纯粹的种族主义行为时，也感到了不安和"痛苦"。一些职前教师甚至告诉我，他们对所看到的态度和行为多少感到沮丧，所以想要重新考虑自己的职业选择。我认为，重要的是要认识到，实际上，不适、愤怒和烦恼也是体验过程的一部分。Bell Hooks（1994：39）回忆起她在多样性、社会公正和歧视方面的教学经历，告诉我们"要放弃旧的思考方式、认知方式去学习新方法可能常常也会有一定程度的痛苦。"我尊重这种痛苦。所以现在我也将对这种痛苦的认知加入了教学内容，也就是说，我教的是改变范式并讨论它可能引起的不适。倘若我们越将这些现象明确地展示给学生，也许我们的教学就会越成功。

问题

1.用你自己的话来解释"简单复杂性"概念。它与跨文化能力有什么关系？

2.通常的（以往的）跨文化能力模型有什么问题？

3.跨文化能力能被测评吗？为什么能或为何不能？

4.你相信有人在想方设法地习得跨文化能力吗？为什么能或不能？

5.为什么我们不能就跨文化能力的“普遍”和“客观”模型达成一致？

参考文献

ABDALLAH-PRETCEILLE M. Vers une pédagogie interculturelle [M]. Paris：Economica，1986.

ABRAMOVIC M. Marina Abramovic：512 hours [EB/OL]. http：//www.serpentine galleries.org/sites/default/files/press-releases/MarinaAbramovi%C4%87PressPackFinal.pdf.

ANDREOTTI V. Actionable postcolonial theory in education [M]. London：Palgrave，2011.

APPADURAI A. Modernity at large：Cultural dimensions of globalization [M]. Minneapolis：University of Minnesota Press，1996.

ARENDT H. The life of the mind：The ground-breaking investigation on how we think [M]. New York：Harcourt，1978.

BACHELARD G. La formation de l' esprit scientifi que [M]. Paris：PUF，1938.

BAKUNIN M. Œuvres complètes de Bakounine（Vol. 7）[M]. Paris：Éditions Champ libre，1979.

BAUMAN Z. Identity [M]. Cambridge：Polity Press，2004.

BENNETT M. J. A developmental approach to training for intercultural sensitivity [J]. International Journal of Intercultural Relations，1986，10（2）：

179–196.

BENNETT M. J. Towards a developmental model of intercultural sensitivity [M]// R. M. PAIGE (Ed.) . Education for the intercultural experience. Yarmouth: Intercultural Press, 1993.

BENSA A. Après Lévi-Strauss [M]. Toulouse: Anacharsis, 2010.

BERGSON H. L'évolution créatrice [M]. Paris: Félix Alcan, 1907.

BERGSON H. The creative mind: An introduction to metaphysics [M]. New York: Kensington Publishing Corp, 1934.

BERTHOZ A. Simplexity: Simplifying principles for a complex world [M]. New Haven: Yale University Press, 2012.

BYRAM M. Teaching and assessing intercultural communicative competence [M]. Clevedon: Multilingual Matters, 1997.

COLLINS P. H. Another kind of public education: Race, the media, schools, and democratic possibilities [M]. Boston: Beacon, 2009.

DEARDORFF D. K. Assessing intercultural competence in study abroad students [M]// M. BYRAM & A. FENG (Eds.) . Living and studying abroad. Research and practice . Clevedon: Multilingual Matters, 2006.

DEARDORFF D. K. (Ed.) . The Sage handbook of intercultural competence [M]. London: Sage, 2009.

DERVIN F. Assessing intercultural competence in language learning and teaching: A critical review of current efforts [M]// F. DERVIN & E. SUOMELA-SALMI (Eds.) New approaches to assessment in higher education. Bern: Peter Lang, 2010.

DERVIN F. A plea for change in research on intercultural discourses:

A 'liquid'approach to the study of the acculturation of Chinese students [J]. Journal of Multicultural Discourses, 2011, 6(1) : 37–52.

DERVIN F. Towards post-intercultural teacher education: Analysing 'extreme'Intercultural dialogue to reconstruct interculturality [J]. European Journal of Teacher Education, 2015, 38(1) : 71–86.

DERVIN F. & HAHL K. Developing a portfolio of intercultural competences in teacher education: The case of a Finnish international programme [J]. Scandinavian Journal of Educational Research, 2015, 59(1) : 95–109.

FRENKIEL E. & ROCCA J. L. La Chine en mouvements [M]. Paris: PUF, 2013.

GALLAGHER S. A philosophical epilogue on the question of autonomy [M]// H. HERMANS & T. GIESER(Eds.) . Handbook of the dialogical self theory. Cambridge: Cambridge University Press, 2011.

HÄRKÖNEN A. & DERVIN F. Study abroad beyond the usual 'imagineering'? The benefi ts of a pedagogy of imaginaries [J]. East Asia, 2015, 33 (1) : 41–58.

HOFF H. E. A critical discussion of Byram's model of intercultural communicative competence in the light of Bildung theories [J]. Intercultural Education, 2014, 25(6) : 508–517.

Holliday A. Intercultural communication and ideology . London: Sage, 2010.

HOOKS B. Teaching to transgress: Education as the practice of freedom [M]. New York: Routledge, 1994.

HOSKINS B. & SALLAH M. Developing intercultural competence in Europe: The challenges [J]. Language and Intercultural Communication, 2011, 11(2): 113–125.

HUNTINGTON S. P. The clash of civilizations and the remaking of world order [M]. New York: Simon & Schuster, 1996.

LAKOFF R. Talking power [M]. New York: Basic Books, 1990.

Levinas E. Totality and infi nity [M]. Pittsburgh: Duquesne University Press, 1969.

LIFTON R. J. The protean self: Human resilience in an age of fragmentation [M]. New York: Basic Books, 1993.

Louie A. H. More than life itself: A synthetic continuation in relational biology [M]. Piscataway: Transaction Books, 2009.

MAFFESOLI M. Logique de la domination [M]. Paris: Presses Universitaires de France, 1976.

MAFFESOLI M. La contemplation du monde . Paris: le Livre de Poche, 1993.

MATSUO C. A critique of Michael Byram' s intercultural communicative competence model from the perspective of model type and conceptualization of culture [J]. Fukuoka University Review of Literature & Humanities, 2012, 44(2): 347–380.

MCSWEENEY B. Hofstede' s model of national cultural differences and their consequences: A triumph of faith – A failure of analysis [J]. Human Relations, 2002, 55: 89–117.

NYNÄS P. Bakom Guds rug: En hermeneutisk ansats till interkulturell kommunikation och förståelse I industriella project [M]. Åbo: Åbo Akademi University Press, 2001.

Piller I. Intercultural communication: A critical introduction [M]. Edinburgh: EUP, 2011.

SAID E. Orientalism [M]. London: Penguin, 1978.

SAID E. Representations of the intellectual [M]. New York: Vintage Books, 1993.

SHI-XU. Critical pedagogy and intercultural communication: Creating discourses of diversity, equality, common goals and rational-moral motivation [J]. Journal of Intercultural Studies, 2001, 22(3): 279–293.

SIMMEL G. Journal posthume [M]. Paris: Circé, 2013.

SPITZBERG B. H. & CHANGNON G. Conceptualizing intercultural competence [M]// D. K. DEARDORFF (Ed.). The Sage handbook of intercultural communication. Thousand Oaks: Sage, 2009.

SUBRAHMANYAM S. Three ways to be alien: Travails and encounters in the early modern world (The Menahem Stern Jerusalem Lectures) [M]. Waltham: Brandeis University Press, 2011.

VALETTE R. The culture test [M]// J. M. VALDES (Ed.). Culture bound. Cambridge: Cambridge University Press, 1986.

VALSINER J. Forms of dialogical relations and semiotic autoregulation within the self [J]. Theory & Psychology, 2002, 12(2): 251–265.

VAN DIJK T. A. Communicating racism: Ethnic prejudice in thought and talk [M]. Newbury Park: Sage, 1987.

WATKINS M. Invisible guests: The development of imaginal dialogues

[M].Putnam: Spring Publications, 2000.

WOOD P. Diversity: The invention of a concept [M]. San Francisco: Encounter Books, 2003.

第七章 结 语

摘 要：结语部分对本书的主要内容作了总结。首先，Edward Said对知识分子的定义被用来重新定义“跨文化主义者”在教育中的角色和地位，比起“专业跨文化主义者”，笔者更推崇“业余跨文化主义者”这一立场。在这一章，我还提出了跨文化教育的十条戒律。这些戒律能更容易地引导读者“测试”自己对本书所提出的理论和方法的掌握程度。

以SAID对知识分子的定义为模型

让我先比较Edward Said对知识分子的研究。在一系列有关知识分子定义的演讲（1993年）中，Said回顾了知识分子的两种类型，对我们如何看待跨文化性的讨论很有参考性：专业知识分子和业余知识分子，两者中他更偏向后者。接下来，我将借用Said对这两种类型的描述，并将它们应用到跨文化世界中（专业跨文化主义者和业余跨文化主义者）。请注意，这两者都是理想类型，因为没有人只属于其中一种。我们每个人都是介于这两者之间的。有些时候，我们可能比业余的更专业，或是比专业的稍逊一筹。

以下是Said对专业的定义：

> 我认为专业素养的意思是，将知识分子的工作视为谋生，在朝九晚五的时间里，一只眼睛盯着时钟，另一只眼睛盯着自认为是适当、专业的行为——不兴风作浪，不逾越公认的范式或限制，让自己具有市场价值，最重要的是体面像样，因而是没有争议、不具政治性和“客观的”。（1993：55）

综上所述，专业的跨文化主义者不惜一切代价避免争论和/或批评；他/她毫不质疑地“坚持”公认的跨文化范例和相关“权威”；他/她还通过循环利用文化差异、二分法等方面的话语，为跨文化想象工程做着贡献；他/她力求尽可能客观；他/她利用跨文化性作为控制自我和他人的“技术”；他/她无视有助于跨文化讨论的跨学科讨论；他/她轻易接受拟人化的概念，例如文化、社区、宽容、尊重、东/西方、第三文化孩子、移民、多样性、融合和复杂性；他/她仅相信（文化）差异，对行动主义不感兴趣，也不期望通过自己的工作为社会正义做出贡献。

业余的跨文化主义者代表着本书所展现的理想立场，我们应该尽可能多地将此作为我们的主要目标，但要记住我们不能总是遵循这种模式。Said这样定义业余：

> 今日的知识分子应该是一个业余者，认识到做有思想、负责任的社会成员意味着他们有权在最有技术和最专业化活动的核心提出道德问题，尤其是在牵涉到自己的国家、国家权力以及国家与公

> 民、国家与其他社会沟通方式时。此外，知识分子作为业余爱好者的精神可以深入并改变我们大多数人习以为常的职业惯例，使其变得更加活泼和激进。他们做任何事情都不只是按部就班地做，而是会追问，人为什么要做这件事，这样做对谁有益，怎样做能够与个人计划和原创性思想重新联系起来。（1993：61）

因此，业余的跨文化主义者将道德和伦理思考放在实践/工作的中心，并且毫不犹豫地承认他/她没有所有问题的答案。他/她超越了常规和被动；他/她还质疑意识形态和道德判断，因此对差异性和相似性感兴趣，并且回避了比较的危险；他/她意识到沟通与情境的符号暴力，以及指导跨文化的权力差异；他/她意识到跨文化是一种简单又复杂的现象，并试图从现实主义视角来对待它。再次引用Said（1993：23）的话："业余跨文化主义者的整体存在由批判性支撑，他们不愿意接受简单的公式或现成的陈腔滥调，或是听起来无比顺耳的权威或传统言论和行为。"作者Taiye Selasi对记者评论的回答很好地证明了这一立场。记者问她："我读到你不喜欢被问到你来自哪里。"她在回答时解释说，这个问题会带来其他"更难面对的讨论"，比如"你为什么在这里?"（2015：n. p.）。业余的跨文化主义者质疑这样的"正常"问题，挖掘隐藏其后的意识形态和态度，而不仅仅是"在这里拧紧语言上的螺丝钉，又在那里松开文化的螺栓"（Shi-xu，2001：287）。

教育中跨文化的十条戒律

戒律一：杜绝差别主义偏见。

“遇到他者并和他们沟通时，首先要问自己：我和他们有什么共同点?”（Moghaddam，2012，第9章）为此，我们应该杜绝差别主义偏见。差别主义偏见是教育领域的常见观点，它只着眼于差异，尤其是与“陈腐的”、普遍化的文化概念相联系时（Abdallah-Pretceille，1986）。其中的偏见之一是个人主义和集体主义“文化”的二分法，通常用来解释“西方”与“东方”人民或“北半球”与“南半球”人民之间的交际。Holliday（2010）对这种差异主义可能引发的民族中心主义和道德评判进行了有力的分析。如果不加节制、不顾语境，继续使用这些元素的话，很可能“轻易地、有时甚至是无意地导致文化低劣的外国他者的减少”（Holliday，2010：ix）。

戒律二：远离个人主义偏见。

关于自我和他人（身份建构）的论述是在人与人之间共同构建的。身份得以创建和存在是因为存在另一个可以比较或与之相对的身份（Bauman，2004）。因此，当跨文化的参与者以及研究人员和实践者在研究跨文化性时，他们的刻板印象、表象和意识形态会影响跨文化交际，从而影响身份（Holliday，2010：2；Dervin，2012）。我的身份是基于他者的存在，反之亦然。因此，我们需要考虑到所有参与跨文化交际的人来解释和理解它们，而不仅仅考虑其中一方。

戒律三：跨文化的失败是正常现象，我们可以从中学习。

不是所有的一切都可以用“跨文化”来解释，因此在研究跨文化时我们也不可能穷尽答案，这一想法尚未在教育中取得广泛认同。然而，我们研究或教导的许多现象都来自游戏、虚构和想象，不可能总得到合理的解释（Maffesoli，1985）。

戒律四：着眼于特例、不稳定和过程，而不仅仅是结构。

许多研究都专注在结构上，专注于描述特定人群（通常由“国籍”或“民族”决定）如何与另一人群进行交流（Piller，2011），导致了“你对他们的习惯和想法越了解，就越有能力‘控制’它们，从而以适当且毫无问题的方式进行沟通”这样的观念。许多学者认为这不能反映当前的“大杂烩”（Pieterse，2004；Wikan，2002），并敦促研究人员和从业人员着眼于特例、不稳定和过程，它们是社会性“天然”的一部分（参见Baumann，1996；Bensa，2010）。

戒律五：考虑到交叉的重要性。

交叉性是指“多种身份的相互作用以及排斥和从属的体验”（Davis，2008：67），它对教育的跨文化有很大启发。这在跨文化教育领域已经是非常普遍的做法，受到批判性多元文化教育的极大影响（Banks和McGee Banks，2009；Sleeter，1996）。许多学者认为，引导相互作用的不仅是“文化”，还包括性别、年龄、职业、社会阶层等共同建构的各种身份。所有这些身份在跨文化互动中相互交错，因此需要全部被考虑在内（Sleeter，1996）。

戒律六：将正义置于教育跨文化的中心。

我还想提出正义的概念：“通过发展理解、态度和社会行动技能，致力于消除不平等、种族主义和性别歧视以及所有形式的偏见、压迫和歧视。”（Räsänen，2009：37）文献中已经发现了一些例子：例如，在Holliday（2010：48）的批判性世界主义范式中，他建议提高人们对制度和文化种族主义及权力结构的认识。

戒律七：举一反三。

在处理教育中的跨文化时，把我们自己的感受、经历和成长经历带入其中。通过增加新的知识来源，举一反三可以提高我们对跨文化的理解和解读。

戒律八：注意权力差异。

权力概念在教育跨文化中应该居于中心位置。无论愿意与否，跨文化的每次交际都取决于与权力关系相关的语言使用、肤色、国籍、性别以及社会地位等。跨文化交际的典型是基于热情好客的观点。Jacques Derrida（2000）通过“敌意盛情（Hostipitality）”这一概念，提出热情好客（hospitality）很容易变成充满敌意（hostility）。实际上，主人和客人之间天生就存在着权力的不平衡，后者受制于前者。

戒律九：语言使用是教育跨文化的关键。

不管是否研究跨文化性，研究都需要使用一种或多种语言，以及非言语形式的交流（模仿、沉默、手势等）。忽略这些要素的重要性是有问题的。例如，当我们翻译一本书中的采访或摘录之类的内容时，我们必须解释某些短语、单词、代词等的选择缘由，因为，任何词的使用绝不是无辜的。我们还需要记住，语言的使用是非常政治性的，它常常会传递权力差异和符号暴力。

戒律十：挖掘背后隐藏的东西；穿透话语表面和表象。

这可能是本书最重要的信息。我们都受到跨文化独特视野的影响，比如它的含义，它如何发生，出于何种原因，等等。我们认为的跨文化现象，或者被视为具有跨文化性的，通常隐藏着我们需要解构、批判甚至重构的元素，以创建更有意义的互动。因此，当我听到文化、社区、价值等词，或一个国家的名字时，我开始反思这些词的使用以及它们对我和对话者会产生什么样的作用。然后我尝试深入穿透话语的表面和表象。

我希望这本书能够激励和启发学生、同僚、从业者和决策者，为他们在教育的跨文化中遇到的有趣且重要的问题提供新的答案。我希望能够激发读者对跨文化进行“逆向思考”，深入研究对话，打破学科和语言的界限。

北京，2015年11月29日

参考文献

ABDALLAH-PRETCEILLE M. Vers une pédagogie interculturelle [M]. Paris：Economica，1986.

BANKS J. A. & MCGEE BANKS C. A.（Eds.）. Multicultural education：Issues and perspectives [M]. New York/Chichester：Wiley，2009.

BAUMAN Z. Identity [M]. Cambridge：Polity Press，2004.

BAUMANN G. Contesting culture：Discourses of identity in multi-ethnic London [M]. Cambridge：Cambridge University Press，1996.

BENSA A. Après Lévi-Strauss [M]. Toulouse：Anacharsis，2010.

DAVIS K. Intersectionality as a buzzword [J]. Feminist Theory，2008，9（1）：67–85.

DERRIDA J. Hostipitality [J]. Angelaki：Journal of the Theoretical Humanities，2000，5（3）：3–18.

DERVIN F. Impostures interculturelles [M]. Paris：L'Harmattan，2012.

HOLLIDAY A. Intercultural communication and ideology [M]. London：

Sage, 2010.

MAFFESOLI M. La connaissance ordinaire: Précis de sociologie comprehensive [M]. Paris: Librairie des Méridiens, 1985.

MOGHADDAM F. M. The omnicultural imperative [J]. Culture & Psychology, 2012, 18: 304–330.

PIETERSE J. N. Globalization and culture: Global mélange [M]. Lanham: Rowman and Littlefi eld Publishers, 2004.

PILLER I. Intercultural communication: A critical introduction [M]. Edinburgh: EUP, 2011.

RÄSÄNEN R. Teachers' intercultural competence and education for global responsibility [M]// M.-T. TALIB, J. LOIMA, H. PAAVOLA & S. PATRIKAINEN (Eds.) . Dialogs on diversity and global education. Bern: Peter Lang, 2009.

SAID E. Representations of the intellectual [M]. New York: Vintage Books, 1993.

SHI-XU. Critical pedagogy and intercultural communication: Creating discourses of diversity, equality, common goals and rational-moral motivation [J]. Journal of Intercultural Studies, 2001, 22 (3) : 279–293.

SLEETER C. E. Multicultural education as social activism [M]. New York: New York University Press, 1996.

WIKAN U. Generous betrayal [M]. Chicago: Chicago University Press, 2002.

必读书目

这里我简要地列出了一些文章和书籍，我认为如果你们想要更多地了解本书所倡导的跨文化理念和价值，这些阅读材料会很有帮助的。这些材料按照作者姓名的字母顺序排列。

ABDALLAH-PRETCEILLE，M. 跨文化主义 —— 思考多样性的范式（Interculturalism as a paradigm for thinking about diversity）[J]. 跨文化教育，2006，17（5）：475 - 483.

Martine Abdallah-Pretceille是法语地区跨文化教育中最具影响力的学者。虽然她出版了许多有趣的法语书，但没有一本被译成英文，但却被译成葡萄牙文、韩文和阿拉伯文。在这篇文章中，Abdallah-Pretceille通过说明文化概念是“过去的事”来总结她对跨文化性的主要论点。她建议我们关注各种各样的文化片段，而不是文化的整体性。她提出文化性（culturality）的概念来代替文化，以体现其灵活性、动态性和变化性。

BAUMAN Z. 身份（Identity）[M]. 剑桥：政体出版社，2004.

这本小书是根据社会学家Zygmunt Bauman和意大利记者Benedetto Vecchi之间的对话写成的。这本书很好地介绍了Bauman的作品，以及他提出的液态现代性的有趣概念，液态现代性象征着我们的时代。社会学家解释了在当今身份的时代，我们的身份是如何经历不断变化的过程的。

BERGSON H. 笑：关于喜剧意义的文章（Laughter：An essay on the meaning of the comic）[M]. 纽约：凯辛格出版社，1900。

Henri Bergson是20世纪一位非常受欢迎的法国哲学家。他的父亲是波兰人，母亲是英国人。虽然他在作品中从未使用过“跨文化”这个词，但我认为他的作品在反思当今跨文化性时是非常重要的。《笑》是他最早的几本书之一，某种意义上很好地总结了他的“过程”哲学。在书中，Bergson探讨了喜剧引发笑的过程，它的社会角色和（集体）想象力的功能。他认为，漫画让我们意识到生活的僵化，由此产生的笑声促使我们从灵活性和对话性的角度看待事物——这是我们倡导的跨文化交际方法中的两个关键术语。

BREIDENBACH J. 和P. NYIRI. 文化无处不在（Seeing culture everywhere）[M]. 西雅图：华盛顿大学出版社，2009.

在这本书中，Breidenbach和Nyiri揭示了文化的概念，并表明我们倾向于系统性地误用和滥用文化来标记和解读差异、误解和冲突。作者提供了许多有趣的例子，说明这一点是如何在不同的情境中形成的。这是一个非常有说服力的呼吁，呼吁放弃与跨文化教育相关的概念！

HOLLIDAY A. 跨文化交流和意识形态（Intercultural communication and ideology）[M]. 伦敦：Sage，2010.

在这本优秀的书中，Adrian Holliday建议从批判和反思的角度来审视“跨文化”。这包括消除跨文化一词在不同用法中带来的强大的意识形态。Holliday为我们提供了许多有趣的例子来证明他的观点。

KRUMER-NEVO M. 和 Sidi M. 以写作对抗他者化（Writing against

otherings）[J]. 定性调查，2012，18：299 – 309。

这篇文章由以色列的两位学者撰写，文章质疑了研究者在撰写关于“他者”的文章时所面临的他者化的潜在危险。作者讨论并举例证明了可以帮助我们对抗他者化的文本机制，比如使用叙述、对话和反身性等方式，这样研究人员可以在写作中分享自己的感觉、经历和历程。

SAID E. 知识分子的代表（Representations of the intellectual）[M]. 纽约：古典书局，1993.

这本书探讨了当今知识分子的含义。虽然它不直接涉及任何跨文化主题，但它与那些有意成为跨文化工作者并有所作为的人是密切相关的。东方主义概念之父 —— Edward Said认为，知识分子必须是不墨守成规的人，他们将批评主义置于团结主义之上，为被边缘化的人发声。为了加强跨文化观点的运用，Said推荐的路径是非常有价值的。

SEN A. 身份与暴力：命运的幻觉（Identity and violence：The illusion of destiny）[M]. 新德里：企鹅出版社，2007.

在《身份与暴力》一书中，诺贝尔经济学奖得主Amartya Sen对当前简化主义的单一身份政治持批评态度，这种身份政治常常导致“我们vs他们”的两极分化以及战争和暴力。他认为，人们太过频繁地根据单一的身份标识（阶级、宗教、性别、文化等）来划分群体、集体和/或社区，而实现和平的关键之一就是拒绝这些观点。

SHI-XU. 批判教育学和跨文化交流：创造多元、平等、共同目标和理性 — 道德动机的话语（Critical pedagogy and intercultural communication：Creating discourses of diversity，equality，common goals，and rational-moral motivation）[J]. 跨文化研究杂志，2001，22（3）：279-293.

杭州学者Shi-xu对跨文化接触和交流的主流教学法提出了最好的批

评。他建议从（文化、语言、翻译）以知识为基础的方法转向以权力、统治、排斥和偏见为中心的观点。

WOOD P. 多样性：概念的发明（Diversity：The invention of a concept）[M]. 旧金山：伊康特出版社，2003.

多样性的概念经常与跨文化性联系在一起。作者在对多样性论述的剖析中表明，这个概念往往是毫无意义的、肤浅的，更重要的是，它是一种两面派的意识形态，像病毒一样在全世界蔓延。

关键术语定义

加速全球化进程（Accelerated globalization）：纵观历史，我们的世界经历了多次全球化浪潮。当前的全球化是快节奏的，拜技术创新所赐，当前的全球化压缩了时间和空间。

综合能力（Agency）：独立思考和表达自我的能力、做决定的能力，和在特定环境下独立行动的能力。

分析型刻板印象（Analytic stereotype）：利用刻板印象作为研究和/或接近某人的基础。例如，根据国籍选择研究对象是一种分析型刻板印象。

人类纪（Anthropocene）：人类活动对地质条件和过程的改变。

拟人主义（Anthropomorphism）：把人类的特性赋予概念、对象和现象。

包法利主义（Bovarysm）：假装比别人好。

文化主义（Culturalism）：用文化来解释代表另一个国家的人的所有思想和作为等，而忽略了可能还有其他原因的事实。文化主义还包括以文化为借口、以文化为托辞的思想。

对话主义（Dialogism）： 在我们所说的每一件事中，总有一个声音是我们以前听过的，我们或明或暗地引用过。因此，说的话往往是对他人所说或所问的回答或评论。有些声音可以被清楚地识别（比如，她说过……）或无法识别。

差异主义偏见（Differentialist bias）： 当我们想到来自其他“文化”的人时，我们总是会认为他们与我们不同，而不是相似。

多样性（Diversities）： 我们每个人都有不同的身份、不同的性格。因此，在欧洲语境中，“多样性”一词是复数形式，而不是单数形式。

本质主义（Essentialism）： 把自己和/或他人限制在单一身份、单一故事（“他们的本质”）。

民族中心主义（Ethnocentrism）： 认为自己的文化、国家或群体比别人好。

欧洲中心主义（Eurocentrism）： 让人认为欧洲处于学术工作、文化生产、和平进程的中心，对欧洲进行盲目崇拜。

脸面工作（Facework）： 当我们与他人交流时，我们需要保护自己的脸面，也就是说，要确保自己受到尊重和善待，就像我们尽力保护对方的脸面一样。

全球本土化（Glocalization）： 一个由全球（global）和本土（local）组成的合成词，用来描述全球现象和本地现象相互影响的过程。

霸权（Hegemony）： 具有强大的象征意义和强大的经济和政治影响力。

阶序人（Homo hierarchicus）： 人类的特征之一是需要创建等级秩序并将人、事物和思想进行分类。

敌意盛情（Hostipitality）： 一个由热情好客（hospitality）和充满敌意（hostility）两个词组合而成的词，翻译过来就是：热情好客中不可能没有潜在的敌意。

右派纲领（Human rightism）：带有偏见与局限、以西方为中心的观点和对人权的解读。

想象（Imaginary）：一种理想化的、虚构的，对某个人、某个地方、某个想法和某个观点的往往负面的印象。

想象工程（Imagineering）：一个由想象（imaginary）和工程（engineering）组成的合成词，用来描述系统地虚构一个人、一种现象或一个物体的某种方式。

个人主义偏见（Individualistic bias）：一种分析跨文化的带有局限性的方法，只考虑牵涉其中的某一个人，而忽略他们的所作所为都是基于在场其他人的事实。只有通过相互交流，才会产生跨文化性。

交错性（Intersectionality）：为了使跨文化性更加复杂，需要将性别、职业、社会阶层和年龄等身份标记与“行为”文化、国家身份和语言进行交叉研究。

雅鲁斯观点（Janusian perspective）：雅鲁斯是个双面神。雅鲁斯式跨文化研究方法通常是矛盾的。它既表现出对一个群体的刻板印象，又表明这个群体的成员具有多重身份，从而消除了刻板印象。

融合（Mélange）：混合的同义词。文化融合是指一种文化受到另一种文化的影响和改造，是跨文化交际中的规则而不是例外。

现代性（Modernity）：现代性到底从何时何地开始，一直争议不断。一种理论认为它起源于1789年的法国大革命。现代性标志着个体、民族国家以及人文和社会科学的诞生。现代社会开始前，上帝被认为是统治人类的力量。当路易十六作为上帝在人间的代表在巴黎被砍头时，上帝也同时被消灭了。人们必须开始对自己是谁、对发生在自己身上的一切负责，并解释/理解他们周围的世界。

国家品牌化（Nation branding）：在世界政治经济中推广宣传国家的趋势。通过国家品牌化，国家可以决定并明确其具体特征。国家品牌化通常被认为是新民族主义的形式。

西方主义（Occidentalism）：将西方想象成一个与东方对立的意识形态之地。

东方主义（Orientalism）：将东方想象成一个与西方对立的理想而刻板之地。

他者化（Othering）：用刻板印象、表象和偏见把自我和他人变成“他者”。他者化往往导致世界等级分化。

夹子社区（Peg communities）：具有21世纪特色的社区。夹子社区本质上是不稳定的，有需要时聚在一起。社区成员之间没有预定的牢固关系。社交媒体是此类社区的典型。

后现代性（Postmodernity）：现代性之后或与现代性交织的时期。后现代性是以身份多重、社会纽带松散和质疑真理为特征的时代。另一个特点是为应对后现代性的不稳定本质而出现的极端主义。

简单复杂性（Simplexity）：一个由简单（simplicity）和复杂（complexity）合成的词。作为对当前世界的一种现实描述，简单复杂性指的是这样一个事实，即我们每个人都必须将社会性当作既简单又复杂的现象去体验，必须在一直简单和复杂的两极之间摇摆。简单复杂性也意味着不可能完全达到复杂性或完全达到简单性。

腹语（Ventriloquation）：通过非语言因素（如手势、面部表情等）重复、表演和模仿别人说过的词语、语段。

仇外（Xenophobia）：对异族、陌生人和差异的仇恨。